T0028311

'Annette is a rare heroine whose fi
an unusual, and beautiful, account of her life. She stood out
in life and this epic will ensure that she is honoured in death.
She deserves nothing less.'

Anne Sebba, author of *Les Parisiennes: How the Women of Paris
Lived, Loved, and Died Under Nazi Occupation*

'The power of Anne Weber's story is equal to the power of her
heroine: it is breathtaking how fresh the old form of the epic
sounds here and with what lightness Weber condenses the life
story of French resistance fighter Anne Beaumanoir into […]
a story full of hardships, which Weber tells with effortless
discretion and subtle irony.'

Judges' citation,
Winner of the German Book Prize 2020

'A riveting and highly original retelling of the life of Annette
Beaumanoir.'

The Bookseller

'[Anne Weber makes] the warmth and vibrant energy of a
unique, very individual life palpable.'

Die Berliner Zeitung

'A reading delight from start to finish.'

Die Süddeutsche Zeitung

'A bold and moving exploration of the ethics of heroism, […]
it pushes linguistic, narrative and genre conventions to their
limits, while posing big ethical questions, as its heroine's ide-
alism comes up against dirty realpolitik.'

The Times Literary Supplement

I

THE
INDIGO
PRESS

EPIC
ANNETTE

A Heroine's Tale

ANNE WEBER

Translated by Tess Lewis

THE
INDIGO
PRESS

THE INDIGO PRESS
50 Albemarle Street
London W1S 4BD
www.theindigopress.com

The Indigo Press Publishing Limited Reg. No. 10995574
Registered Office: Wellesley House, Duke of Wellington Avenue
Royal Arsenal, London SE18 6SS

First published in Great Britain in 2022 by The Indigo Press

First published in Germany in 2020 as
Annette, ein Heldinnenepos by Matthes & Seitz Berlin

A CIP catalogue record for this book is available from the British Library

ISBN: 978-1-911648-45-1
eBook ISBN: 978-1-911648-46-8

This book has been selected to receive financial assistance from English PEN's PEN Translates
programme, supported by Arts Council England. English PEN exists to promote literature
and our understanding of it, to uphold writers' freedoms around the world, to campaign
against the persecution and imprisonment of writers for stating their views, and to promote
the friendly co-operation of writers and the free exchange of ideas. www.englishpen.org

The translation of this work was supported by a grant from the Goethe-Institut.

Cover design by Luke Bird
Art direction by House of Thought
Cover photo (left) by permission of the estate of Anne Beaumanoir
Cover photo (right) © Hermance Triay
Author photo © Hermance Triay
Translator photo © Sarah Shatz
Printed and bound in Great Britain by TJ Books Limited, Padstow
Typeset in Goudy Old Style by Tetragon, London

Supported using public funding by
**ARTS COUNCIL
ENGLAND**

Annette Beaumanoir died on 4 March 2022,
two years after this book was published in Germany.

Anne Beaumanoir is but one of her names.
She exists, indeed she does, not only in
these pages, but also, to be precise, in Dieulefit,
a village – 'God-made-it' – in south-eastern France.
She does not believe in God, but He no doubt believes in her.
And if He does exist, then surely He made Anne.

She is very old but even so, as this story goes,
she is not yet born. Today,
at the age of ninety-five, she comes
into the world on this blank page –
into an impenetrable void in which she peers around
blindly like a mole as the emptiness
gradually fills with forms and colours,
father mother heaven water earth.
Heaven and earth are fixed phenomena
but water comes and goes, it flows
into the Arguenon's dry bed, where twice a day
it sets upright the boats that have been stranded
on their sides for hours. Twice a day

it retreats into the sea, a channel in these parts
called *La Manche*, the sleeve, for short,
although it's neither a channel nor a sleeve,
nothing hollow, more of an arm, in fact:
the arm the Atlantic reaches towards
the North Sea. The boats resettle
gently on their bellies.

In the universe of this room, still uninhabited,
swim four and sometimes six
glittering stars or eyes. As in a darkroom,
contours emerge slowly from the void
and faces begin to form
around the stars. Mother. Grandmother.
Father. The child, whose name is Anne but everyone
calls Annette, sets these planets in motion.

Today's Anne is twice as far removed
from Annette in years as her
grandmother was then, and yet somewhere,
immensely far and near,
this child still exists. She and the child are one,
the latter neither withered away nor dead,
but asleep, still there.

Annette was born in a dead end
and not just metaphorically
as we all are. Her grandmother's house is the last

in a row of crudely built fisherman's cottages that
ends abruptly at the river. Each small cottage
has a living room downstairs and upstairs,
right and left, two attic rooms.

'Her grandmother's house' does not mean
that it belongs to her. She's a tenant. As a residence
it's beggarly and accordingly the rent is low,
but low as it is, it's high for her,
a young widow raising three children
on what she earns from *pêche à pied*, or
gathering seafood by hand: day after day
she sets out at ebb tide
to scour the damp sand for any kind
of sea creatures – clams, shore crabs,
carpet shells, whelks – which she lugs
in a basket on her back to nearby
villages – to Saint-Éniguet, La Ville Gicquel,
Le Tertre, Notre-Dame du Guildo,
or Le Bouillon – and sells them there.

Her mother's mother was born in the nineteenth century
in Brittany (and so in a certain sense in the seventeenth),
to indigent peasants who, unable to feed
their many children, placed them
one after the other in service to the better off.
The little milkmaid is very poor. For a long time
– her young granddaughter was later shocked to learn! –

she wears no underwear. She has none. Sleeps on straw. Her
yearly wages are a new pair of clogs, and every other year
either a cloak and socks or a skirt and jacket, hardly
a luxury because she's not yet full-grown. She never
goes to school. *Illettrée* is what they call those who, like her,
can neither read nor write. At fifty, it suddenly
occurs to her – Annette must have been seven at the time –
that not once had her mother ever kissed her and she,
who has never once complained, bursts into tears. And so
they sit together, grandmother and granddaughter,
and they kiss and kiss and kiss
and weep. All she remembers of her father
is his brutishness. She never mentions her siblings,
child farmhands and maids like her.
Perhaps they've died or disappeared,
or perhaps they live nearby. Annette
loves this grandmother above all else, a woman
whose wealth is immaterial and whose knowledge
does not come from books.

Like each of us, Annette has a second one,
a grandmother she loves less.
This is her father's mother, a Beaumanoir,
which means 'handsome manor house' and, in fact,
theirs is *the* best family in the area,
a place without the better sort.
Madame Beaumanoir, also widowed, is
the daughter of a notary. Annette never once sees

Grandmother Two in her first years.
The bridges between her and her son were burned
the day she forbade him to marry the girl
from the fisherman's cottage – one of Grandmother One's
daughters – surely a source of pain for
Madame Beaumanoir, but what was she to do?
Every fibre of her being opposed
the unequal union, from which, to her chagrin,
an Annette soon issued. She takes her son
for something better and she's not wrong,
he is a better sort, since he renounces both
her respectable company and his inheritance
for the sake of his love. At this point
the lovers are still nearly children, not legally
of age, and therefore require parental permission
to marry, and so Annette is born – as in a Breton
fairy tale – in Grandmother One's poor fisherman's cottage,
outside the bonds of wedlock but well within those of love.
As for a birth certificate, well,
that would come later.

One could call her parents happy,
but is that true or, generally speaking, even possible?
Isn't it always said that happiness is at best
a fleeting state? But her parents are happy,
always so. Let anyone with proof to the contrary
speak now. Joy is the basso continuo
of their daily life. Suffused with this inaudible,

warming music from the very start and
endowed with her parents' clear eyes
and intrepid hearts: enter Annette.

Annette's parents are not only happy, they're also
opposites: night and day. Jean is tall and
Petite Marthe is short; he is measured and composed,
she a lively chatterbox but sensible, too,
and on top of that a captivating storyteller. In short,
she is the whirlpool, he the rock. His favourite
nickname for her is 'my suffragette', inspired
less by her feminism than her tendency to sputter with fury
and indignation in the face of injustice.
She's the type that Bretons call *soupe au lait*,
her temperament like those soups that boil over in a flash.
In such cases, Jean is the one who gently lifts the lid.
She taught herself everything she knows and while *everything*
may not be absolutely everything, it's still a great deal:
the joy of reading, say, or the art of ping-pong. Only driving
eludes her, tempestuous as she is.

No wonder, one might well conclude, that in such
favourable circumstances their daughter became
what she did, which the book jacket
can hardly summarize with so little space for a wealth
of decades actions events trouble.
If it were true that circumstances alone determine
our futures, we'd be relieved of all responsibility,

all sense of guilt, all pangs of conscience. But
life is not that simple. The essential task
lies before us; it must still be done.

At this point, Annette is almost five; her birthday
is coming soon, but will she live to see it? This is,
in retrospect, a stupid question, but the answer
at the time is far from certain. For she is ill,
deathly ill, not even conscious.
But she finally comes to and the first thing she sees
is the bicycle that was her birthday present.
The Great Depression has just begun, but her parents
have taken no notice; they've weathered a deep depression
of their own, at their only daughter's bedside,
not praying but following with desperate precision
the orders of a doctor, who himself does not believe
the child can be saved.
Cerebral meningitis. Finally, the worst
is past. Annette is conscious but not yet herself;
her recovery doesn't happen overnight. It's a long,
slow process she still remembers
ninety years later: first she felt her muscles
skin joints tendons and intestines
return to her, and only when her ears, too,
came back could she hear her parents' voices.

A summit meeting between the two grandmothers
is held at the convalescent's bedside.

Madame Beaumanoir meets La Mère Brunet,
as Grandmother One is called in the village.
Delighted, yes, both are absolutely *delighted*,
mainly to see their little granddaughter
recover. Annette's parents
are by now of age and married.
From now on Annette will bear her father's name;
also, of course, that of the reconciled Grandmother Two,
at least on paper: Raymonde Marcelle Anne
Beaumanoir. She has long since left
the fisherman's cottage and moved with her parents
and Mémère across the iron bridge that spans the
    Arguenon,
the Pont du Guildo, which Mémère's husband,
an ironworker, had come here to build
only to die, five years and three children later,
of TB. The new house, a cottage too, is on the other bank,
across from the house in which she was born. At low tide,
all that's left of the river that separates the two houses –
a mighty waterway at high tide – are two rivulets.

What happy homes, someone standing
on the bridge today might think at the sight
of the two cottages on either bank. In the hallway
of the second, evenings before dinner, the family
plays football between the front door and
her parents' bedroom door
until the tenth goal is scored.

After dinner they wrestle, in happy homes
a sign of, well, happiness.

When a dance is held on the bridge below,
Mémère and Annette dance the polka
in the kitchen at the open window.
Although Annette's father, Jean, is a socialist,
the pastor – we are in Brittany
and the clergy, of course, is Catholic –
Monsieur le curé, then, often comes to dinner,
which is hardly surprising, once you know that
his first act as parish priest was to equalize
all the candles in his flock, at least by size.
Before that, for first communions – depending on
how rich their parents were – one child carried a candle
no bigger than a finger, while another
 – the young Dibonnet, for example –
marched like a bishop behind a veritable pillar of wax.
Naturally, Jean gets along well with this priest
and to avoid causing him any worries,
he has Annette receive first communion
(Annette's mother, Marthe, is hardly pleased,
but she, too, is fond of the priest). This gives rise
to two weeks of 'explosive mysticism'
(in Annette's words), which is not nothing, to be sure,
but compared to the nearly hundred years
that have passed since then, it's not much either.
Before and after: nothing.

In the village, as in Dumas's fiction,
there are the blues and the whites,
the republicans and the royalists, that is,
but the latter aren't really royalists,
although they are conservative
and Catholic. For their part, the blues
are still republican and, what's more, they're secular,
which means they want the Church separate
from their personal lives, of course, but especially
from the State and without any say if possible.
In Brittany, such wishful thinking
is considered an impure thought. In Saint-Cast
there are two girls' schools. One is Catholic, which
most of the children attend, even the daughters
of the few well-off peasants and those of the tenant farmers
on the ducal estates, for there is a duke
and, therefore, a castle too. The other school, run by the State,
is filled with the daughters of the poor, even destitute
sailors *au long cours*, on long-distance hauls,
to catch tons of cod off Newfoundland and bring it back
months later as stockfish, dried and salted.
There are daughters of coastal fishermen, too,
along with two, three peasant children,
thirty girls in all, a small knot of secularism.
Annette learns to read and write there and,
as soon as she's figured out how,
she starts teaching Mémère, who

never learned to do either.
The cave under Annette's duvet is an ideal
classroom, and after a few months both can read
or at least decipher. With Annette's help Mémère
writes the memorable phrase: Today
I made soup with leeks and potatoes from the garden.
For her son-in-law she reads out loud – haltingly,
but still – a definition from the dictionary.
Which word it was is unfortunately unknown.
Nonetheless it's clear: under the covers,
the word 'Enlightenment' still means something.

A quarter of a century later, Annette's grandmother
lies dying. Annette is at her bedside and,
in order to bear the parting, she grips
the book she is currently reading,
that is, not actually reading, just
holding. It's Arthur Koestler's
Darkness at Noon, and the cover
of the French edition reads *Le Zero
et l'infini*, nought and eternity:
the two titles take on a new meaning
in the dying woman's room.
The declining woman stretches an emaciated
hand towards the book, looks at it
for a long time and, the trace of a smile
flitting over her lips, points her thin,
gnarled finger at the *z* of *zero* and in a soft,

slightly mischievous tone, says: I never could
remember that one.

Pause.

Back to the beginning, because Annette's
life has only just begun. As has been noted,
in 1929 she already owns a bicycle,
which not every five-year-old can say, especially
if their parents, like Annette's, are not well off.
Still, not every child her age
is the daughter of a champion cyclist,
well, champion is an overstatement,
but of an athlete nonetheless, who rode in
the Tour de France in the early 1920s,
before Annette was born.
Later, on the Quai du Guildo, beneath the house
on the bridge, he will open a shop promising
bicycles and small agricultural machines.
He will also be the only one in the village,
no, actually one of two, to own an automobile,
which he basically uses to drive
various neighbours here and there because
Le Guildo had until then suffered the lack
of a free taxi. In winter, a bit further along the same quay,
a circus family lives in three covered wagons, people who
used to be called gypsies or, in French, *romanichels*.
Annette's father repairs their unicycle and anything else

of theirs with wheels for free. Annette
likes to play with their daughter – with one of their daughters –
even though Mémère insists that she
has lice. If the Pope himself had claimed otherwise,
she would not have believed him
and she's the only one in the family
who believes anything he says.
Mémère tries in vain
to keep their two heads apart
and gently works a fine comb through
the little girl's hair before spoiling her with crêpes.
It's clear the three generations and four people
of the Beaumanoir family are good neighbours,
in fact, the best you could hope for, and
the gypsy women bless them from morning to night.

Like their parents, the children in school
are divided in two: those from the land
and those from the sea,
the peasants and the sailors,
those who gurgle with words and
those who, next to them, seem civilized.
All who live near the estuary, even
if they don't set sail, are turned
towards the open water.
The tide brings small cargo ships
up the river that must be unloaded
quickly, before the water retreats.

Often sailors leap ashore speaking
languages not a soul here understands, but this
doesn't prevent anyone from talking to them. *La
     maîtresse*,
the primary school teacher, is the widow
of a merchant naval officer whose ship and crew
were swallowed by the north-west Atlantic
off Iceland. Every morning, the teacher herself
stands unswallowed in front of the class,
in which two little girls, both named Germaine,
are equally bad students but the *maîtresse*
only yanks on one of the girls' braids
as punishment. Which of these
might be the mayor's daughter?
Annette owes her early, acute sense of
injustice in part to this first
teacher's decisive influence.

Annette is then enrolled as *interne*
in the *collège* of Dinan, the state school
for children eleven and older. *Interne* means
that she boards at school and can only
go home every two weeks to visit
her parents and Mémère. On the school bus
she makes eyes at a boy named Jean-Baptiste – at least
that's what she calls him, she doesn't know his real name.
She gives him that name because he's thin and has

dark curls just like John the Baptist. An early start!
But the pseudo-saint takes no notice of her.
Or at least he pretends he doesn't.

At twelve in 1936, she spends
her last summer in her parents' house
by the sea. *Mais qu'est-ce que c'est que*
tout ce monde? What in God's name
are all these people doing here? (In her mind,
God is merely a turn of phrase.)
The socialists and communists have instituted paid
holidays, a mere two weeks, but still,
long live the Popular Front! Crowds spill out
of local trains, minibuses – out of anything
with wheels. They brandish fishing nets
and spades, clad in holiday garb,
which is nothing more than their Sunday best
blackened by the soot of steam locomotives.
They are everywhere, singing, playing ball.
What once was seafront is now
a broad popular front. For the locals,
these summer visitors, wherever they come from,
are all Parisians, that is, from the capital,
in other words, as good as capitalists.

Summer 1936. Everyone knows what's going on
in Germany. Mussolini rules over Italy.
The Spanish Civil War begins.

To a twelve-year-old in Brittany it all seems
further away than Syria or Sudan does to us today.
But appearances deceive, because the first Spaniards
are appearing, Spanish women, to be precise.
Their husbands dead, wounded or in prison,
they've come to Brittany with their children,
seeking refuge. Annette no longer boards at school
since her parents left their house on the estuary
for a home in Dinan, where they assist
the Spanish refugees and run a café-restaurant,
which is essentially nothing more than
the welcoming committee which they've joined
out of a sense of honour and kindness. Annette
is a pacifist until she decides at fifteen
that she'd rather be a terrorist. Reading Malraux's
Man's Fate, she is very taken with
Chen, one of the characters who, in 1927,
during an uprising of workers and communists,
moves from killing others to killing himself.
Chen is driven by the idea of sacrifice, even if
said sacrifice is a complete failure, like his own
suicide bombing in which he stupidly dies,
missing his target. So do men live by dying.
By dying for others? Or by wanting to die,
wanting only to die? Chen's death wish
saves him from dying against his wishes,
thus sparing him *man's fate*.

Malraux is awarded the Prix Goncourt and is later
named Minister of Cultural Affairs, neither of which
keeps him from acquiring a dubious reputation.
Regardless, his reputation isn't our concern.
Annette's enthusiasm is, her passionate attachment
to the idea of devoting her life
to a cause, a purpose, an ideal. In 1938, the first
German refugees arrive, one of whom is named Elsa.
'As a German, she was, prima facie, an enemy.
Still, she was very pretty' (in Annette's words).
Elsa's from Berlin and rarely speaks
because her French is bad, but it's good enough
to understand a thing or two: that people here
don't trust her, for example. So she tells of an uncle
who was lynched in his own shop by a few brutes.
No one doubts her words.

Then begins a war that, at least in France,
is not a real one, rather it's a period
of waiting or sitting still, a time the French
call *la drôle de guerre*, oddly enough,
since there's nothing amusing about this 'funny war'.
Not that the French have a better sense of humour
than their neighbours, but they're hardly adept
at foreign languages, so instead of *phoney war*,
it seems they hear *funny war*.

The unfunny war finally breaks out as well.

The offensive begins on 10 May 1940 and
is over by 22 June. The Germans advance
like a knife through butter and for the French
eighty years later these six weeks – mere weeks,
not even months! – still rankle. By July the Germans
are marching in goose-step through the streets
of Dinan. They now make the laws. Annette
is sixteen and wants to see them up close.
It's here and now, in these weeks,
that something clicks inside her, unless,
that is, it happened much earlier
at the estuary of the Arguenon.

When the tide comes in, the river puts up
resistance. The highest and lowest tides
come twice a year in spring and early autumn.
The strongest are called *les vives-eaux*,
living waters, and the turbulence where
sea and river currents collide can throw up a wall,
a moving dam of water, a tidal bore
they call a mascaret.

It starts with small steps. Annette is sixteen,
it's summer, and someone addresses her,
a man. A new romance, perhaps? Possibly, but not
this time. He is S, a prisoner of war who,
with two other prisoners, is led around the city
to translate for the military command. The three

are not closely watched and S is able to exchange
a few words with Annette as she passes. Could she
collect several small packages near the wall
of the former barracks – now a prison – and
take them to the address written on
the smallest one? (It's the only real address. The others
are made up.) Would she be willing? Well,
what do you think? That's right: of course she is.
At the real address lives a lovely, courageous
seamstress who can create things out of nothing,
and so all the more out of this package. She has braided
her blonde hair into a crown and once led, rumour has it,
une vie de folie, a wild or, rather, racy life in Paris,
where she bore a son, now a prisoner in Germany.
Annette sees S two or three more times
before he escapes, to London, she learns years later.
He leaves her a copy of *L'Espoir* (*Man's Hope*),
another novel by Malraux, this one about
the Spanish Civil War, which S experienced first-hand,
along with a few other books as gifts,
then he disappears. Annette meets other
members of the Resistance, a primary school teacher,
for example, for whom she delivers
packages on her bicycle here and there
throughout this summer and the next. Like many things,
active resistance is different than one imagines,
that is, it's not one clear and final decision
but an imperceptibly slow slide

into something still unknown. First
and foremost, one must resist one's own self.
And one's own fear. What if she were stopped
while carrying forbidden documents or goods? She learns
that fear can be overcome.

A year passes and Annette is still so young.
If only she could grow up a bit more quickly.
How much longer will this dreary and, for her,
much too uneventful, period last? She wants to act,
but is always told that she's too young.
What a bore! Half-heartedly, she begins
her medical studies in Rennes
while dreaming heart and soul of a destiny full
of great sacrifice and heroic acts.
Only the opportunities are missing. Thanks
to the schoolteacher she has a few 'contacts',
not like the contacts we share today
with everyone we meet, but a small group
of trustworthy people with the same
or similar covert intentions. But when
will things get serious? Why doesn't anyone
entrust her with an important mission? When will
these *verdigris*, as they call the German soldiers,
finally be chased away? And why don't
the streets of Rennes look like those in Canton
during the revolution in *The Conquerors*, yet another
novel by Malraux? When will the revolution come?

The enemy is only incidentally German Nazism. Its true face
is imperialism, capitalism and nationalism.

For now, all there is for Annette to do is wait and
ride her bicycle. A minor mission takes her
to central Brittany, to a hamlet near Uzel,
a place so small and inconspicuous that it
can no longer be located at all. There's already
one bicycle in the shed; strange, it looks
just like her father's… unless it's… Well,
there he is. So he… too? Jean makes it clear
that no one, not even her mother, Petite Marthe,
needs to know of their chance clandestine meeting.

All this is well and good, but
not nearly adventurous enough.
'It's inhuman' (Annette's words) to leave
hanging for so long someone who
has decided to risk her life
for a distant future, no, not even for
a future but for an ideal, for something
out of reach. At university she finally meets
C, a committed Trotskyite, who sends her
to a meeting in Brest, where, no surprise, it's raining.
The blue-black uniforms of Nazi Germany's navy
melt into the night. Annette turns
from one dark street into an even darker one,
knocks four times then twice more on a door,

and says: Dinan here! as instructed.
She is Dinan, the worthy embodiment of her city.
The curfew obliges all those present
(a few men and three women aside from Annette)
to stay there, talking, until dawn. The result,
written more or less in German, is a call
on the *verdigris* soldiers to distance themselves
from the brown shirts and black coats.
How is that? Do these night owls really think
they can convince German soldiers
to desert? To renounce their government?
Could they be any more naive?
There's a park in Dinan where the German infantry
likes to stroll, and Annette is meant to distribute their flyers
there. But to her disappointment (and our luck)
she waits for their delivery in vain. Empty
promises! Such audacious and ridiculous initiatives
lead to the arrests of several in her circle
in the summer of '42. Caution demands – and surprisingly,
even Annette occasionally obeys – that she
leave Rennes. In any case, she longs
for serious action and for some time has been eyeing
the Communist Party, outlawed since September '39.

'If you don't have any strong convictions at sixteen'
(in Annette's words), 'there's a good chance
you never will' (in non-Annette's words).
We close our eyes to death and terror and all

that usually follows revolutions, 'we hope for the best
and go full speed ahead' (the rashness is Annette's),
towards a place that doesn't exist and never will,
a place where peace, freedom and fraternity don't
rule so much as… prevail. This place is, no doubt,
not called Paris, yet that is precisely where
Annette now lands and is, before long, back in action.

Her room is on Boulevard Kellermann,
named after an Alsatian who conquered
the Prussians at Valmy with General Dumouriez.
On this boulevard in September '42 – now, that is –
there is a factory, roughly across from Annette's,
with the name Gnome et Rhône, which almost evokes
a sense of Franco-German friendship. In fact,
aeroplane motors for the German air force,
specifically for the Messerschmitt Me 321,
are produced there. Annette's mother
is not exactly pleased with her daughter's
new address, but Annette won't be there long.
She is studying medicine and so far has
made only one acquaintance in Paris. She
is called Mona Lisa. Parisian students are quick
of tongue and their minds are just as fleet,
so they always seem to have understood far more
than they have left to learn. In no time at all
they can sum up what they've grasped
into thesis, antithesis, synthesis,

then, with a bundle of foreign words as kindling,
they set alight a stunning bonfire. This talent
is more or less innate, so it would be unwise
to take one's own measure from them.
Annette doesn't even try: her tongue
seems made of lead.

Is her destiny now finally taking shape?
If so, then we know the presiding gods: they're called
Jean, Mémère and Petite Marthe, they're called
Arguenon, fisherman's cottage and changing tides.
Paris is big! Paris is small. Tiny, in fact,
if you only count those who refuse to fall into step
with the Germans and go on as before, who are restless
and ashamed. And this small band of recalcitrants
never show themselves or recruit others,
you have to want to find them and know how.

Annette finds them with her fishing skills –
la pêche à pied! – she knows it well.
On Boulevard Raspail, she notices an active group
of young people led by Marc Sangnier, whom she
suspects of resistance. He who fishes shall find!
She's met one of them previously and he
puts her in touch with a *contact*. Chance
or destiny leaves very little margin for error
in this first encounter: on one particular side
of a certain stairway in the Jardin du Luxembourg

she will see her contact leaning on the railing,
immersed in a book and, clamped under his right arm,
Signal – not the brand of toothpaste we have today,
but a propaganda journal spreading Nazi ideology
in the occupied countries of Europe. She is to say,
'What a lovely spring day!' Not in German, of course,
but '*Quelle belle journée de printemps*' – hardly suspicious,
but not exactly a natural way of speaking either.
Or maybe that is how Parisians talk? It's unlikely
that anyone is watching them. They sit on a bench,
nothing unusual in the Jardin du Luxembourg.
He is surprised at the youth and inexperience
of this new recruit they've sent him. She doesn't
know the city or even how to type. Is she
at least ready for a *lâcher* or a *collage*?
Of course she's ready – but what exactly do
collage and *lâcher* mean? He looks at her: am I
supposed to fight the Nazis with mere children?
Fine. In fact, maybe not such a bad idea. The girl
looks harmless, far more harmless, no doubt,
than she actually is. The man is correct and
in more ways than one, but at the moment
he's thinking of *contact* only as connection,
not as touch. He doesn't offer her his hand,
just precise instructions: Tomorrow evening at six,
corner of Rue Mouton-Duvernet and Avenue d'Orléans.
Wear the exact same outfit. A man in a cap will ask
how to get to Rue de l'Odéon and you'll say:

33

'The day after tomorrow.' Annette listens to him
without thinking, as we do, of certain
black-and-white films with similarly absurd
dialogue. Instead, she thinks of tomorrow
and of her contact's slender, nervous hands.
They stand up and walk together to Place Denfert-
Rochereau, where he abruptly orders Annette:
'*Traverse!*' And she crosses the street. That's all.

Enough for today. Now she'll have to pass tests
that have nothing to do with medicine. In Rennes
she wrote slogans on walls and delivered packages
that were much too heavy to hold only documents.
Annette also knows how to use a mimeograph. Her next
steps are: *collage*, putting up posters at night, and
lâcher, which requires crowds of people into which
one plunges before scattering three or four bundles
of flyers over one's shoulder or dropping them (*lâcher*).
This has nothing to do with *lâche*, or cowardice;
the two words are simply homonyms. Another action
that is not for cowards is standing up in a cinema
at the very end of the film, when the audience
is preparing to leave, and shaking them up through
a megaphone. 'Countrymen…!' But for that you need to know
every inch of the spaces and how to seize
the right moment. She's good at both.
Only once does someone grab her legs,
some gnome or collaborator, but since no one helps him

34

and Annette is quick and a former future gymnast,
she slips out of his grasp and is gone.

Her mentor is satisfied with her and
with good reason; he waits for her beside a kiosk,
behind an open newspaper. They set out,
as if without a goal or with a goal
not marked on any city map, and she need not
cross the street. Still no instructions.
Place de la Contrescarpe, Maubert, the bank of the Seine
to Pont Marie, which has spanned the river for centuries.
And the two of them? They stand there for the first time.
A sweet silence gradually descends on the bridge as the sun
revolves around the lovers, adorning them as if…
Their combined ages are forty and tomorrow
they may well no longer be alive.

He goes by Roland, at least for now – no one has
kept their original name. His is Rainer
Jurestal, originally Juresthal with an 'h'. A Jew
of German ancestry who grew up in the Paris suburb
of Saint-Ouen, now called *banlieue nord* or
Quatre-vingt-treize, i.e. ninety-three, not referring
to 1793, the year of the Terror and the Revolution,
but to the postcode, the code of those who come
from elsewhere, who are not French or not French
enough. Roland is a member of the political
youth movement Jeunesses communistes, and Annette

will soon join too. Status: permanent combatant
in the underground, a *clandestin permanent*;
indeed, life in the underground can go on a long time,
if you survive. What does change is all the rest:
sites of actions names lodgings. Now he's Roland
Vergne, now Roland Fleury. First she's Odile,
then Carré and then Soyer. Their hideouts, or
planques, are on Boulevard Bonne Nouvelle and
in Asnières, quite a distance outside the city limits.

They are now lovers. Is this permitted?
The communists have not made any allowances for love,
or rather, they have and decreed it strictly forbidden.
And with good reason: every personal relationship
brings risk. Each *clandestin permanent* knows only two others,
no more, no less, and only by their false names. If caught,
betrayal is impossible, even under torture. The two lovers
are clearly violating the Party's rules, but they are not
    concerned
because, as everyone knows, there are things no party,
no person, nor any law can prohibit. Of course, the 'cadre'
    must not find out,
but how could they? Their entire life is now clandestine,
a cupboard bursting with secrets, which holds yet one more.
When choosing their hideouts, they opt for those
with a double bed; there's one in Asnières, where
Annette is staying. She knows that her Roland,
young as he is, has already lain, a husband,

36

in a conjugal bed. He was married at nineteen
to a girl just turned eighteen. With his wife and her parents
he had tried to cross the demarcation line.
Just as refugees fleeing Somalia or Eritrea do today,
they gave all their money, everything they owned, to a smuggler
who knew or was supposed to know how best
to reach the other side. The smuggler told them
they had to cross a river, the Creuse perhaps,
or maybe the Cher, not knowing or even caring
that her parents couldn't swim. They stayed behind
and were arrested. The newlyweds did not get far.
As soon as the young Sophie stepped into the water,
she was shot – by German guards, no doubt –
while her husband, Roland, was able – by diving
underwater? – to climb ashore downstream,
unfortunately on the wrong bank.
What he tells Annette later is everything he knows
about the death of Sophie and his in-laws. What he
probably never learned, a fact someone found
seventy years later on a French government website,
is that Sophie Jurestal did not die on a riverbank but
in Auschwitz. In the river, the bullets must have
only grazed her. She was pulled from the water alive,
sent to Drancy, and on to the death initially begrudged her.
This thin, white paper gravestone shall bear her name and
dates:

> *Sophie Jurestal, born Hammer*
> *Warsaw 11.1.21–19.9.42*

Pause

Resistance is normally aimed against
a specific force, in this case German tyranny
and its hate-filled ideology. In certain situations,
those resisting may be more inclined
to question whether a given rule or regulation
is just or justified. Consider this example:
if our two rebels still have a bit of meat
on their bones, it's thanks to the provisions
Jean and Petite Marthe send each week, not
directly to one of their *planques*, of course,
but alternately to one of two addresses
where friends of theirs live. These parcels,
filled with Mémère's Breton delicacies,
smell delicious. One January day in 1944,
Annette collects one of these care packages
from the Bs, on the ground floor of a brick building
near the city limits. Madame B's name
is Elisabeth and she is a concierge. Her husband
works at the Hachette messaging service, where
he has learned that there will soon be a *rafle*,
a round-up of the Jews, in the 13th arrondissement,
in a district called Butte-aux-Cailles. Elisabeth
knows that another concierge there, a woman
named Victoria, is hiding, in an attic, a few Jews who
narrowly escaped the last *rafle*. The orders this time
are to search every inch of every house.

They don't stand a chance. They have to leave.
They have to go, but where?... 'Annette? Annette,
you know people, you have to let the leaders
of the Resistance know!' Annette smiles. She nods.

Before she goes, she promises to do everything she can.
Everything she can! What, exactly, can she do?
What can her leaders do? This woman, Elisabeth,
seems to think the Resistance is an organization
for saving persecuted Jews. Lost in anxious thought,
Annette hurries down Rue du Moulin de la Pointe,
then along Avenue d'Italie. She pictures,
scattered throughout the country, even across
the entire continent, sheds cellars lofts filled with
crouching, haggard-faced people waiting for her.
No individual actions, she had sworn
to the Party. No initiatives. She is just a cog
in the wheel and her only job is to turn.
Every day she risks her life in actions
planned by others. She has accepted
this subordinate role; she agrees that it
is necessary. Individual plus spontaneous equals
danger. She would like to help,
but is not allowed. If she were caught during
an impulsive action, she would put the organization
at risk. Hang on… She raises her head… Isn't
Butte-aux-Cailles nearby? What's the name of that street
to the left…? Rue du Moulinet! Somewhere

on this street a Jewish family is hiding in an attic.
Annette stops. For several wild heartbeats she weighs
the odds, considers various hiding places and rejects them.
She thinks of Roland. Then she walks to the entrance
with determination and knocks at the door
of the concierge with the self-assured name
of Victoria. As they climb the stairs, the concierge tells
Annette who is hiding there: Mr Lisopravski,
an upright man, a widower with two grown children.
Until recently, he had run a bakery on Rue
du Moulinet, along with his deported employee's
young wife. They've all been hiding here since
the bakery was demolished months ago.
The door opens. To Annette, the father seems old
for a father and the children seem tall for children.
They are, in fact, taller than Annette, although slightly
younger. The girl is fifteen or sixteen, the boy seventeen.
The young woman is pale and holds an infant
in her arms, whom no one had mentioned and who now
must be saved as well. Five people! And she alone,
Annette, with her still doll-like features, is now
responsible for them all. 'You'd better come
with me, you're in danger here,' she tells the man.
The father looks at her sceptically. Is he really
meant to entrust himself and his loved ones
to this child? Annette stands in the doorway, trying
to look confident, but the man examines her warily
and doesn't answer. Instead, he asks the concierge

if she knows this young woman. Victoria,
who has known Annette barely five minutes longer than he,
says: yes. The father and his children have an agitated,
anxious conversation in Yiddish – Annette
doesn't understand a single word – surely about
whether or not they should leave and, if so, with whom.
The young mother seems to have no will of her own; her eyes
dart back and forth between the trusted man and
the intruder, Annette, who feels the young man's piercing
gaze on her as well. He must be wondering who
this unknown girl is who has arrived out of the blue
and wants to save them for no apparent reason
other than that she, like they, is a human being.
The father is distrustful – she needs no words
to understand this much. She can hardly blame him.
In his place, she would be too. He must be wondering where
the girl could hide so many people. Even if she wanted to,
which she does. The father and the children convince
each other. He hugs his daughter tightly and repeats her name,
'Simre, Simre.' He cannot decide and yet he must. Finally,
he lets his children leave with Annette. He stays behind
with the young woman and her baby. Perhaps he believes
his children's chances of surviving are better without him?
Without the young woman and her child? Could he
have left this woman, who now has no one else,
is on her own? Is she perhaps now more to him than just
the wife – more likely the widow – of his employee?
Is he too old, too tired, to follow this girl,

fearful and horrified, through the occupied city and
go to ground in some dubious new hiding place?
The door has closed behind the three some time ago,
but he stands immobile, face buried in his hands,
wanting only to weep and weep and weep,
and we, in a distant time, are moved and unmoving,
unable to find any words or sentences or lines
that could begin to comfort or explain.
We stand with him and weep.

Three human beings stay behind in the attic room,
three others make their way to the underground,
the Métro, not the Resistance. At the entrance
of the Tolbiac station, Annette's glance falls
on the yellow star that gleams like a golden target
on the girl's lapel. It must be torn off right away.
Neither of the two grown children – she is Simone
and he Daniel – dares, but Annette
persuades them, and the obscenity is ripped off
and all three board the train, not in the last car,
which the Nazis have allotted to two of them,
but in the middle car. It is eight o'clock. The train
departs. Everything seems to be going well,
although not in Annette's mind, crowded as it is
with doubts and fears that are swelling
in waves of anxiety. How can she be sure
that the news of an imminent round-up was true?
How does she know the two children weren't safer

in the attic than in this Métro car? What if they
are caught and killed because of her impulsive eagerness
to help? A siren cuts through the bad air,
the train stops and the loudspeaker orders all passengers
to leave the Métro and be off the streets within
thirty minutes. The curfew has been brought forward,
something no one could have predicted.
The train has stopped at Havre-Caumartin,
a half-hour on foot from the city limits, and Asnières
is another half-hour's walk from there.
Let's stop a moment and think – no, there is no time
to think, and in any case they have no choice.
They have to leave and trust in chance, which may
or may not wear a German uniform. Annette doesn't
think of 'the Germans' or German uniforms as a whole.
She can distinguish between the poor soldiers
drafted without a say, and the SS. Besides,
the man to whom she has given her heart
and soul has German ancestors – not something
that can be changed on the orders of
an ephemeral regime. Be that as it may, at the moment
she'd much rather walk than think, but that will offer little
consolation: the curfew is close and Asnières still far.

Annette, not long out of childhood herself, leads
the two children through the night. They
reach the *portes de Paris*, the old fortifications,
and don't know if these gates will open

onto a new future or onto death. The January
wind is icy in these outer districts where the houses
are sparse, but the three walk quickly, as quickly
as they can, and so at least they suffer the cold
a little less. They dart across empty squares and
along unlit, empty streets, three silent ghosts
whose thoughts are directed towards one goal
but whose bodies are not equally trained. For months
Annette has been crossing the city from north to south
and east to west, so she doesn't tire easily, but the children
haven't had a childhood filled with running
and jumping – there was no room for that in hiding,
nor any space for laughing or scuffling. Annette
gives them furtive sideways glances, searching
for staunch words to give them courage,
but is so scared and skittish herself that words
escape her. Was it really her duty to abduct
these two young people, to tear them
from their father? They hurry through the thick,
dark night; they plod on and make no progress,
at least that's how it feels. And suddenly
a silhouette emerges from the motionless dark,
a man approaching on two wheels, quickly enough
for them to tell, if not who, at least what kind of man
he is, a German, riding a bicycle confidently
through the night – and he doesn't see them
or perhaps prefers to forget them on the spot.
Annette silently thanks this man and

the bicycle too, then she thinks of her father
and Petite Marthe, because she knows
without having to ask that they will take in
the two children. This gives her new courage.
But first, the three of them must make it all the way
to Brittany! They've arrived at the large curve the Seine
makes as it winds indolently out of Paris, and on the bridge
Annette hesitates once more as she weighs
whether she should be prudent and go ahead alone
to make sure the coast is clear and to draw up a plan
with Roland on how best to proceed. After all,
their building may be watched. There's a *commissariat*
nearby, filled – like every other French police station –
with snitches and agents responsible
for dealing with what they call 'Jewish affairs',
but that is just a cover for accessory
to murder. Maybe she could bring the children to
that dog cemetery where she and Roland
use an old gravestone for the dog Fidèle
as a hiding place for keys and papers? But she
decides against it. She won't leave the two of them alone.
Here is the house, here the stairs. They leave behind
the cold fog rising from the river. Roland is home
and without asking many questions, he agrees.
And somewhere, beyond the city gates,
almost in the great beyond, there is a man, who
for a short time – hours, weeks? – will remember
Simone and Daniel as his beloved children.

The children will live, they must. Once at home
in Asnières, Annette thinks of the third child, the baby
in its mother's arms in the attic on Rue du Moulinet.
She thinks how all those hidden there
are going to be arrested that very day,
the baby too. And she thinks of another baby,
her own, hardly even a baby yet, asleep in her womb.
A love child, as they say, who never will be born,
because this is no time for children, it's time to fight,
in Roland's view. And in her view, too,
at least she'd like to agree with him and fight
at his side, but there's a war inside her as well,
and her body, lined with another, resists the joint decision.
But they are resolved. She could still shake their resolution,
perhaps, but it will stand firm. An appointment
with an angel-maker has been made. And even if her hesitation
doesn't last, something else inside her hesitates that night
when, in tears, her arms around Roland's neck,
she tells him of another child, the baby on Rue du Moulinet,
and of the distress in its mother's dark eyes. Should she
have been more insistent, described the dangers
more vividly? Annette believes, she hopes,
that she did everything she could.

The baby, the one left behind, still hangs
by a thread in the world of the living on this night,
and only years later will it learn of this thread,

spun by Annette from her head to Roland's.
The following morning, Roland sets out to try his luck
on the Rue du Moulinet. Who knows, maybe
the round-up hasn't reached them yet, maybe he
can persuade the hesitant young woman
to let him at least save her baby if they won't save
themselves. Luck is on his side. Roland finds all three:
Simone and Daniel's father, the young mother and her child.
Does she still hesitate? Or does some instinct make her trust
this young man who probably speaks her mother tongue?
Does knowing his girlfriend inspire her trust? In any case,
moments later, the young man walks down Rue du Moulinet,
the baby in his arms. The very next night, just before dawn,
the two adults hiding in the attic are arrested and
what happens next is murder.

But there's one thing no amount of torture or even death
can undo: because the young mother could not let her child
go when Annette appeared in the doorway, because she held
her baby tight and would not release it, Roland appeared
the following morning and he not only could save her child,
but could also assure Daniel and Simone's father
that his children had safely crossed Paris and now had a
      chance
to experience again the wind and sun, rain,
sorrow, joy, all that he would soon be robbed of,
dreams, actions, passions, games – life, in short.

Moments later, then, the young man walks down Rue du
    Moulinet,
a baby in his arms. First, he brings the child to Asnières and
places it in the arms of Annette, who, for a few hours,
will be both mother and big sister. But the baby
cannot stay. So Roland takes the infant to people he knows
working day and night to find shelter for Jewish children.
The little girl – for she is a girl – is saved. On the same day
Roland and Annette save this child, they lose another,
their own, still floating, not yet conscious, in her womb.
For everything there truly is a season,
a time to bear children and a time to resist, and
these two are incompatible. On this day of salvation,
Annette digs her own child a grave in her heart.
She, who does not believe in God or in angels,
surrenders this tiny life, this minuscule being,
to one of those women who, time out of mind,
have populated heaven with them.

It is done in the morning. That afternoon,
shortly after leaving the woman's house, instead of
taking a moment to recover, Annette boards a train,
home to her parents' house in Dinan, where she hopes
her wards Daniel and Simone will be harboured
for a time. Not wanting to be seen, she arrives
after dark. But in case she should, nonetheless, be seen
and recognized, she has put on a nurse's smock.
However, all such precautions are no help

if everything does, indeed, have its season, since
there is a time to inform on others, too.
Still, Annette's faith in her parents was well placed.
There's not a shadow of hesitation or doubt
in their eyes when she unexpectedly emerges
from the night, hugs and kisses and asks them.
Annette's father accompanies her to Paris
the next day to help her acquire forged papers
and fake train tickets. Annette is away from Asnières
for only one brief night but that's precisely the night
an SS troop comes stomping up the stairs,
a many-legged monster, in search of new prey,
which it finds easily. At this point, certain events occur
that we are tempted to call Providence; it's as if,
at the very last minute, someone, in whom
no one truly believes any longer, ever so slightly
moved a lever and changed the tracks of fate.

On the former track, when we last looked,
four people were hiding in the room in Asnières:
Daniel and Simone, Roland – and Annette, away
for just that one night with her parents in Dinan.
These four could or should have been arrested then.
And now the slight but critical shift in tracks: not far
from her *planque* the day before, Annette
bumped into Marcelle, a young woman she knew,
who'd come running around the corner at full speed,
like a madwoman. At first, she wanted to hurry on,

but when she recognized Annette, whom she'd met
somewhere two years before, Marcelle breathlessly
told Annette that the police (French) had come and
arrested her father, that her mother and her young son
had watched it all from the neighbour's garden, that
she now had to intercept her husband Bernard,
who would arrive at Gare Montparnasse
with provisions the next day, and warn him
not to go home. Before she finished telling
Annette all this and a thousand other things,
they were already in Annette's room because
she'd naturally – naturally? – taken in the harried woman,
as she would Marcelle's forewarned husband
the following day. They are now six people
hiding in the one small room. But Chance
or the supreme pointsman decreed that the very day
the SS pound up the stairs and Annette is away
happens to be the two newcomers' wedding anniversary.
Their fourth. And that for this occasion, Roland
would borrow a key to a room on a lower floor
where a friend of his prints illegal newspapers and flyers.
To give the young couple one night alone,
without three others in the same room,
Roland and the two children decamped
to the floor below, where they heard the SS troops
storm up the stairs and bang on the door above
at five o'clock in the morning. Yet on that very night
Roland, Annette and the two children are not there.

In their stead, the married couple are found in the double bed
and arrested. The three one floor below save themselves
by jumping out of the window onto the roof of a cinema,
then leaping over a narrow gap and into a garden,
where they cower in a small shed for hours. *Raus! Raus!*
The soldiers' baying reaches them. They have only
their pyjamas, nothing else. How can they leave the shed
unnoticed? A smock hangs on a nail, a smock
small enough for the girl to wear, and there's a pair of shoes
big enough for Roland. But only the girl can wear
both together, smock and shoes, and Roland
sends her out alone in this get-up to get some clothes
from a friend in town. Once in a while, luck holds.
The adolescent crosses town and returns
with a bundle of clothing. The friend who musters
discreet outfits for a man and two teenagers
is the same one who knows how to put an end
to pregnancies. She's also the one who'd organized
the nurse's gown as a disguise for Annette.
A young woman, single, no children – one of many
and yet too few who help whenever and wherever
they can but whose names are now forgotten.

A crazy coincidence no one could have predicted
is that the two newcomers, the young couple
who sought and found refuge with Annette,
unwittingly become the saviours of their saviour
when an improbable chain of peculiar circumstances

put them in the wrong place at the wrong time.
Roland and the children go to ground in a new,
equally precarious hiding place. He warns Annette.
He calls her at her parents' and, disguising his voice,
tells her not to return to her room in Asnières,
now under surveillance, and where to hide instead.
In case someone else is on the line, he
uses code names for every place and each person.
Now, when Annette returns to Paris with
her father, Jean, who is helping her with
the children, the two won't fall into any trap.
Instead, they'll go straight to their new refuge. Jean knows
where to get forged papers and train tickets to Rennes,
but he must return to Dinan before the documents are ready.
Daniel and Simone will have to board the train alone,
but they know exactly where to go in Rennes,
to a bistro right behind the station where they'll be safe
since the owners know Annette's parents.
Jean will collect them in his car, at least that's
the plan. They find the bistro but there's no sign of Jean.
They sit in a back room and wait. They wait for hours.
The owners grow concerned but their own reserves of fear
were used up long ago. Someone finally comes
to collect them, not Jean but Petite Marthe, who arrives
by train since she doesn't know how to drive and
because the Germans summoned Jean, as soon as he returned
from Paris, to a place with a name that inspires terror:
Kommandantur. He is detained and interrogated

about his daughter. They want to know where she is,
what he knows about her and when he last heard from her.
They're searching for Annette, whom they know as
    Raymonde,
and don't realize that in Jean they've landed
a much bigger fish: Jean – and no one besides, perhaps,
Petite Marthe learns of this until the Germans are gone,
no, longer still, in fact, not until Jean's death since he's not
the type to do things so he can boast about them
later – works for the covert organization Gallia,
a resistance network within the intelligence and operations
agency, the Bureau central de renseignements et d'action.
Gallia spies on the German military for London and
Allied bombardments. This is the reason he couldn't stay
in Paris until the children's papers were finished:
he has something extremely difficult to obtain
in the winter of 1943–44, a pass for the forbidden zone,
the *zone interdite*, a broad band along the coast that is
strictly off-limits even to locals. This safe conduct
pass is only valid for a limited time
on a specific day. But on that particular day,
Jean will not be scouting the coast or
collecting the children. Instead, he'll spend
the day being interrogated in the *Kommandantur*,
a three-storey villa called La Caleta, not, as feared,
about his espionage but about Annette.
'I wish you could tell *me* where she is and what
she's up to!' he exclaims. 'We haven't heard from the child

for a long time now. She always used to write or call.
We're very worried.' The Germans don't believe a word;
they've heard this often enough before. They apply
their usual arts of intimidation but he stays calm,
like the candid, upright Breton he is.
The Germans – that is, the few who take advantage
of this place to swagger – believe him in the end.
Or maybe they don't; in any case, they let him go for now.
They will keep an eye on him.

Their place is not exactly ideal for hiding
two Jewish children. But Jean and Petite Marthe
take them in. Perhaps their view is that
in an ideal place there'd be no need to hide
anyone at all. They wait a few days
until the air is clearer or their caution less,
then collect both children from the farmer
with whom Petite Marthe had left them. Simone,
from now on, is a relative from up north
helping out in Jean and Petite Marthe's Café des Sports.
The situation is riskier for the older one, Daniel.
They hide him in a garret and only allow him out
now and again at the break of dawn and only
near the house. This requires luck, of course,
but there's also something else: *ça sent déjà la fin*;
they can smell the end of German rule. The closer
the Allies advance, the more the number
of collaborators and informers dwindles and

the greater the host of *résistants de la dernière heure*,
those last-minute resistance fighters who sign up
when it takes neither courage nor conviction or who know
their futures will be grim if they don't switch sides.
No neighbours denounce the siblings. Daniel can even study
in hiding thanks to a friend of Jean's, a headmaster
who gives him books and a lesson plan.

So much for Dinan, for Jean and Petite Marthe,
for Daniel and Simone. But what about
Roland and Annette in Paris? They are Party members
and discipline is strict. Not only do they receive
no praise at all for their courage or for saving three lives,
they're punished and reassigned. They put themselves
and others in danger. From the Party's point of view,
they were, in their selflessness, resisting the Resistance
and its inflexible order. They are sent to Lyon,
where So-and-so (a pseudonym) will give them
further instructions, but So-and-so does not appear
at the designated meeting place in Lyon that day.
There's no sign of him the next day either
at the so-called *rendez-vous de repêchage*,
the back-up plan – there always is a second plan,
even a third or fourth – for those not infrequent
occasions when someone arrives too late
or cannot come at all. By the third day, it's clear: no one
is going to come. They've been dropped by those in Paris.
And now? Now maybe they could consider whether

they've already done enough. Out of the question.
Their only contact in Lyon is this So-and-so,
who probably doesn't even exist, but Roland remembers
someone he knows in Clermont-Ferrand, someone
from the Resistance, of course. Such fleeting thoughts
can change an entire life, we all know this,
but we usually forget, and by forgetting it, survive.
Roland sets out for Clermont – it's 160 kilometres
away – and finds him. The young man puts him in touch
with an underground movement called Jeunes laïcs
combattants, a youth organization of a Gaullist bent.
The JLC can use them both, as long as one
comes to Clermont-Ferrand and the other stays in Lyon.
They part. How will this work? It works. Is there something
they're more devoted to than love? In this moment,
they would say no, but their actions say otherwise,
so there must be something. They part in Lyon
in the Parc de la Tête d'Or under a tree – a hornbeam,
called *un charme* in French, which may not
possess any charming powers, but the two lovers
still feel enchanted when they see each other
for the last time under this tree.

Those interested can easily learn
that among the many root systems found in nature,
the hornbeam's, in cross section, has the shape of a human heart
and so in German it is also called a heart-root.

Annette and Roland don't think, when they part,
that it will be forever. Who would? They do know
the danger of what they're doing. They live with fear
the way a circus tamer lives with a big cat,
with a tiger, let's say, that he knows well and always
keeps his eye on. Roland and Annette are clever
and they've been lucky, at least until now.

Early in the summer of '44 – two months before
the Germans leave Clermont – Rainer Jurestal,
alias Roland, is arrested on the Place Delille.
He's able to escape from prison the next day
but, along with two other Francs-Tireurs and partisans,
he's captured in a small hamlet called Servières
in the volcanic hills outside Clermont.
A shepherd – the kind of man one might expect to be
a peaceful sort – saw the three fugitives near an abandoned hut
where they'd taken shelter on their way to rejoining
the Maquis. This shepherd – sadly not of men – tells
a local farmer, a certain M, who summons his male
    relations.
They soon arrive, armed with clubs and rifles,
and beat the three strangers. Thrilled to give in
to their cruellest instincts with impunity,
they maul the young partisans. When one of three,
Paul Berquez, tries to escape, a son of Farmer M
shoots him, shattering his elbow.

The mayor of Orcival, the local authority,
tries to intervene, to tame the mob's bloodlust,
but here, as in many other places, the real power
lies with local militias eager to serve the Germans.
The mayor protests in vain. At this point,
at least, let us interrupt the tale a moment, because we can,
and, casting our eyes on them from this distant era,
silently speak their names into eternity:
Paul Berquez, Raymond Stora, Rainer Jurestal.

The Ms, whose existence is so banal, so trivial
that our story and history itself remember them only
with a single letter, one that also stands for Milice française,
these Ms, then, drag their prisoners a few kilometres
away to a secluded place and murder them, each
receiving a bullet to the neck. They bury the three bodies
near a lake now owned by the Michelin firm
as a private fishing spot for their employees.

In that same year, in '44, after the Germans have fled,
the battered corpse of Rainer Jurestal, alias Roland,
is exhumed and reburied in the frigid cemetery
of Saulzet-le-Froid on a high plateau between
the Chaîne des Puys and the Monts Dore massif,
but this time solemnly or at least officially.
Five years later, this man's remains, all that is left
of his slender, engaging person, his meagre shell,
now empty, will be exhumed and reburied

a second time. The last of his restless resting places
is the military section of the Saint-Ouen cemetery,
in the Parisian suburb where, not long before,
he had been a student at the Collège Jean-Jaurès.
The National Office for Veterans and Victims of War pro-
    motes him
posthumously to the rank of Captain, *mort pour la France*,
seemingly forgetting that until then a yellow star
was his only medal from the fatherland
for which he gave his life. This is the fatherland that
deprived him of all his rights and hunted him for years
in order to ship him and his kind on the national railways
to a transit camp and from there to certain death in the
    East.
Mort pour la France? Dead for the fatherland?
Did Roland not die, rather, for a far greater land, one
very unlike his own, a land called Fraternity?

After the German troops withdrew, members
of the M family, who took part in the savage beating
and murders of the partisans, were finally called to account.
The sentence is death by guillotine, but
it isn't carried out. Instead, they initially serve hard labour,
then, after penal labour is abolished in 1960, their sentence
is reduced to imprisonment. Perhaps – very probably, in fact –
they are granted an early release. In any case,
they will now disappear from this book,
which has no intention of offering them shelter.

No ink is dark enough to render
the blackness of their souls.

Annette is alone in Lyon. Roland is far. Before,
she'd received news of her parents now and then
through a third party. Not any more. As the Resistance
and prudence dictate, she has finally cut all ties to her past
and to the future. Isolation is the watchword.
She must be as silent as the tiny fish she is
in the great machinery of the movement,
without acquaintances or friends. If anyone
tries to start up a conversation or asks a question,
she puts them off with polite, evasive answers
and moves on with a preoccupied air. She knows
her few contacts by sight and by their false names;
exchanging anything other than official information
is forbidden. She slips ever further out of the society
for which she has given up her studies, her family and
friends, her lover, and would even give up her life,
although she acts as if she were just like everyone else,
that is, she gets dressed every morning and leaves the house,
or rather houses, in which she lives now under this name,
now under that, and comes home as if from work.
Although she acts as if she had a social life, she is alone
and as lonely at twenty as if she were on the moon.
Like Odysseus on his long journey, seeing his companions
perish, one after the other, Annette is gradually cut off
from her origins and her past. Not one person

she meets in Lyon knows her real name or her history.
She lives in her own shadow. And like Odysseus,
if asked for her name she could truly say: I am nobody.

As if on autopilot, Annette walks the streets of Lyon
without knowing why or to what end. All the instructions
given to the pawns on the Resistance's giant chessboard
are worded so that these small fish have no idea
why they are doing this or that. She must surrender her free
    will,
at least until she herself has a few will-less pawns to direct.
What is it that drives her? Why has she given up her life,
the only one she has, before it has begun? Does she even
    know?
Do we ever really understand why we do what we do?
Reasons to explain her actions are easy to find: who
would want to be terrorized by the Germans, especially
citizens of another land? Wanting to fight against oppression
and against foreign rule, wanting to fight for justice: reasons
enough to join the struggle. Enough indeed, and yet
there might be others. As a fighter with the underground,
she may well have made peace with herself and what she wants
from life. If it's true, as some believe, that we are always
playing a role for others and ourselves, then she is playing
    one
that seems tailored for her and can therefore hardly be
    considered
a role at all but rather is her true self. There is another factor

to consider: the thrill of risk, the adventure, the feeling
of leaving a grey and monotonous existence behind
along with familiar habits and customs. In the hall of mirrors
that is her new life, everything is reversed. What once
was bad – falsehood, let's say, or spying, theft – is now good
simply because the end justifies the means. Furthermore,
the end tends to swell to the disadvantage of the means.
In this dark jungle of a world, filled with predators and
    danger,
Annette swings between euphoria and fear. She is completely
on her own, subject to the thrill of the unpredictable
and the unknown. Paradoxically, this adventurous parallel
    life
consists primarily of waiting and long hours of travel in stuffy,
overcrowded trains, of hundreds of kilometres on foot or
    bicycle,
of hunger and boredom and nights spent in empty,
unheated rooms. Although a few resistance fighters
like to dip into funds sent from London to play the lords
and dance on the volcano, most of the troops make do
with the bare minimum. As does Annette,
who knows no one and who, no longer sure
exactly who she is, is Nobody.

In Lyon, everything becomes more complicated. The various
movements within the Resistance are now all focused
on how the country will be run after liberation
and are jockeying to come out ahead. Annette finally does

meet a contact in the Party, but he officially works for
the Gaullists, for the Unified Movements of the Resistance,
a confederation that includes the three major
    non-communist
resistance movements in the southern zone:
Combat, Franc-Tireur and Libération-sud.
Complicated, indeed! Annette's contact is a communist.
What is this communist doing where he does not
belong? He is spying and he recruits Annette,
not as a 'spy', but as a 'submarine'. She believes
the Party is a force for good and does as she is told.
What difference does it make? Isn't resisting paramount?
And resist she does. Annette is assigned to a cadre
named Porte. This is the narrow gate through which
she must pass to return to the Party's good graces
after having defied its most elementary rules by saving
three Jews. Although she finds it unpleasant, she
complies. Her mission: to become a representative
of the UMR to the FUJP, the patriotic youth movement
Forces unies de la jeunesse patriotique, and to rise
in the ranks as quickly as she can. Undercover,
as a 'submarine' should be, she is to join in,
keep her eyes open and, at the meetings, always vote in line
with the other, the official communist. She endorses
all suggestions made by this representative
of the Front National (at the time the FN was not
the disgrace it is today, but the name of a communist
resistance movement). This all seems strange, and it is,

but perhaps less so if one bears in mind that this is not just
a struggle for power but a cause Annette believes in:
the country's structure when the French rule themselves
again. She's fighting for a future that is as radiant and just
as possible, a future not only without Nazis but also
without capital, or dead labour, as Marx calls it. She is
Nobody, but she has a goal and this goal – no surprise –
is a place that does not exist, or if it does, then only
as a goal: an ideal, a utopia. On her way
to this no-place, she sometimes wonders
if she is serving as an auxiliary to the Reds and
the Partisans or rather as a travelling saleswoman
hawking Charles de Gaulle accessories. The Gaullists
pay her salary, and it is far more than the communists
ever offered. It's a modest amount, to be sure,
but without it she could not make ends meet
as a full-time rep. In any case, it's considerably more
than she has ever earned before. Her faith in the good cause
is so deep that she offers the difference to the Party.
As a result – at least in this one case – de Gaulle
unwittingly provides financial support to the communists.

Another of Annette's duties is to maintain contact
with the Maquis, in those remote mountain regions where,
between assignments, the partisans lead normal lives or,
at least, lives that, compared with hers, seem normal
and convivial. Numbers are ballooning in the mountains.
In the past year, the ranks of true *résistants*, fighting

from conviction, have swelled with those whose main wish
is to avoid being deported as forced labour to Germany.
All of them must be fed. Since the partisans lack
almost everything they need, some of which the enemy
possesses in excess, Annette takes up robbery on the side,
like the night in Lyon when she and a young man
from Romania or maybe Bulgaria, whose alias is Milou
(after Tintin's dog), break into a warehouse near
the train station, where a collaborationist youth group
has been hoarding hiking boots. The problem is
that Annette and Milou can only get in the warehouse
if one or two of the Pétainistes are there. Milou
has brought along a cudgel in case they're spotted.
But no: they're locked in the warehouse that night.
Like bank robbers, they had cased the joint beforehand,
and with the help of a small light they find
the drawer that, according to their informant,
holds the key to the storeroom. Then they must wait
for a signal in the very early hours from their accomplices
outside and unlock the door from inside. The night is long
and seems ever longer, given the strange, unsettling noises.
The doorbell finally rings and they're about to open the
    door,
when they realize there's someone else in the warehouse
and it's definitely not a mouse. But who? And what?
It's some poor sod, a half-hearted Pétainiste, who'd also
hidden in the warehouse intending, like Annette and
    Milou,

to relieve the collaborators of their store of boots.
But in his case, it was not to help anyone but himself. And so,
at twenty, with Milou's help, Annette captures her first
prisoner, who tells them of a second warehouse, filled
not with shoes but with warm blankets. Their selflessness
is a lesson for the prisoner, who learns it so well
that he probably ended the war a 'Hero of the Resistance'
like so many others. At least according to Annette.

There are hundreds of such operations, large and small.
Yet Annette spends most of her time on roads, rails or paths,
in buses or trains, or on foot. For her and her kind,
the many spanners in the Occupation's works,
resistance seems like a very long and tedious journey,
which brings us back to Odysseus. She criss-crosses
the south of France just as she covered every inch
of Brittany and Paris. At the train station in Valence
she waits hour after hour for a train to Lyon, and when
it finally pulls in, she sees that it's filled with Germans
and has one car for collaborators. Nearly paralysed with fear,
she finally boards the train after the stationmaster almost
lifts her in, whispering in her ear that this will be the last
    train
on this stretch for at least two days, because after Lyon
it will derail. He has already informed the gentlemen
on the train – not that it will derail, of course, but that
the young lady must get to Lyon, to start, according to him,
an apprenticeship. Aboard the train she feels like a mouse

in a vipers' nest, only these snakes are clad in felt hats and
leather jackets. Addressed by one of these reptiles,
she is forced to engage in conversation. Will the train ever
arrive in Lyon? Will she be allowed off? She is aflame with
      fear,
for her the compartment is a personal hell. With burning
      fingers,
she shakes the frigid reptilian hand the German soldier
extends to assist her from the train, which derails as planned
some thirty kilometres on, just past Villefranche. This and
      other such
acts of sabotage are what were called 'battles of the rails'.
(At the same time, and without hindrance, French trains
are transporting deportees in cattle cars to the East.)

In her new life underground with the Gaullists, Annette
is astonished at how relaxed their rules are compared to
      those
under the communists, when each resistance fighter knew
just two others and even then only by assumed names.
Things are different for her now, no more triangles of trust.
The rigorous discipline – which she herself didn't always
follow – had advantages, of course: one's life was safer.
Gaullists sometimes gather in groups of ten,
which seems to her extremely risky. She feels as if she has left
the Marxists for the laxists. One day she's ordered
to meet seven others in an apartment in Lyon
on Place Puvis de Chavanne. Only four are told the address.

The idea is that they'll enter by twos in intervals.
A minimal precaution, thinks Annette. When she arrives
at the sleepy square basking in the midday heat,
followed by the young man she is to guide, she notices
some suspicious-looking men on a shady bench who glance
more often at the door through which she and the young man
are meant to slip than at their open newspapers. At the sight
of these men, so different from the elderly usually dozing
on these benches, Annette turns around and, young man in
    tow,
wanders the adjacent streets, hoping to warn any not yet at
the meeting place. They find no one. Two others
share her foreboding and turn around as well.
The remaining four, already in the apartment, are caught
and taken to Montluc, the German prison in Lyon. One dies
under torture in this jail, where Marc Bloch and Jean
    Moulin,
like many others, were imprisoned before them.

While they suffer in prison, Annette picks apricots.
Hard to believe, but that is how it is. Death. Torture.
Or apricots. Not much in between. A bit less wariness
and luck, and Annette might have been dying in Montluc
or some other hole. Instead, she's sent 'to the green', which
sounds rather like a holiday and, compared to her work in
    Lyon,
it nearly is. While she's there, the higher-ups will investigate
whether or not she is somehow connected to the arrests.

At first glance, it looks fishy when someone misses a
    rendezvous
that ends in a trap. And so, in June of '44, Annette is sent
to Provence, where she picks apricots. In that same month,
four others suffer in Montluc, the Allies land in Normandy,
and in Oradour-sur-Glane, the Waffen-SS Panzer Division
'Das Reich' massacres the hamlet's 642 inhabitants. All the
    while,
the lavender blooms, plump cherries dangle, crimson,
on twinned stems. It all takes place at the same time
in the same world as everyone knows, but only
in an abstract sense because distant reality is hazy and,
like a dream, hard to grasp. The investigation
yields no results. After a few days Annette's time
in apricot paradise is up. She is given new instructions
and a train ticket to Marseille.

Bit by bit, she has crossed the length of France and finally
reached the southern end. Born on the Atlantic coast,
or on the Channel, to be precise, she sees, for the first time
and with new blue eyes, the ancient, endlessly blue
    Mediterranean.
That is, she would have seen it if Marseille were not engulfed
that evening in a proper Breton drizzle. Like the rain,
night falls in drops of darkness, and, leaving the station,
    Annette
sees a crowd of odious militiamen, whose only ambition
seems to be exceeding the SS and the Gestapo in baseness.

Her orders are to find a certain ironmonger's (more
easily ordered than done) and address the man
in grey overalls. When she finally finds him,
she can hardly understand a word he speaks
in that rumbling dialect spoken only in Marseille,
the verbal equivalent of sun-beaten iron. Once again,
a new room. A new name. New streets. And this time
even a new language. A new sea. And strange new creatures
that are quite simply, or rather bitingly, bedbugs.
A soapworks in the courtyard. Heat. August.
Stink. The Mediterranean is a beautiful,
garishly painted sister of the sea she knows.
Marseille! It's here the war – *her* war – will end.
Here, she will finally no longer be Nobody. And here,
soon after her arrival, she will learn of Roland's death
from a tall, gracious blonde. It will take decades, more
than seven, for this death and this love to penetrate
her consciousness, to settle there and finally sink
into enchanted slumber like a child never to be born.

In a few days, this city will be liberated and with it
Annette. Grazed by death, she embraces life again
in so far as life also consists of closeness to others,
involvement with and interest in them. She is assigned
a courier, a messenger who is only twenty, like Annette.
This unusually open and trusting young woman
had previously worked for the postal service
(which makes her in a sense a long-time courier)

in a village in the Ardèche. Her name is Chévité,
a name the boundless World Wide Web tells us
is a noble family name from the eighteenth century.
Even so, this young woman from the Cévennes
bears it modestly. Chévité could not stay
in the Cévennes: the Germans had instituted censorship
in her post office as in all those throughout France
and charged her – of all people, who can't tell Roosevelt
from Churchill or from Stalin and who mourns
the abominable collaborator Philippe Henriot,
recently murdered in Paris by MLN, as a hero
of the Resistance – they charged Chévité with the task
of censoring others. A quick aside: Philippe Henriot, also
    known as
'the French Goebbels', a man who despised Jews,
Freemasons and communists, was besotted with butterflies.
The impaled objects of his love can be viewed
in the natural history museum in Karlsruhe. End of aside.
Unsuited as she was, little Chévité would not have lasted
long in the censorship business and worse,
at the end of the war no one would have had any patience
for her ingenuousness or her excuses. So she joins
the Resistance and is soon unconditionally devoted
to her superior – that's the term they used – Annette.
Ideology is not Chévité's strong suit, it's true, and she's not
particularly bright, but it's no coincidence that she
cast her lot with the right side – the side we see as right.
When your heart is in the right place, not in your mouth,

for example, then your head, too, empty as it may be,
is unlikely to go off-track. In any case, through Chévité
Annette recovers the warmth of human ties. Unfortunately,
she must soon send Chévité to Toulon – on the very first train,
in fact – where she is to deliver a small package
to a laundry (actually, just a front). But Chévité
never makes it to Toulon. Instead, they later learn,
she ended up in Avignon. Why is that? On that particular day,
there was only one train, as such both the first and the last,
and it went to Avignon. Miraculously, Chévité found in
    Avignon
a laundry on a street with the same or a similar name
as the one in Toulon, perhaps not quite a laundry,
but a woman doing ironing. She gave this woman
the package and she, in turn, gave Chévité something to eat.
That is Chévité. Ten years later, she has become a nun,
developed a faint moustache and gone to Africa
to tend victims of leprosy.

But before all this can happen, Marseille and Toulon
must be liberated. The Allied forces have landed
in Normandy. On 15 and 16 August 1944,
they attack on the southern front. Thousands of soldiers
dangling from parachutes waft gently to the ground
along the coast: a beneficial plague of locusts for which
many here have desperately wished. Thousands of ships
approach the coast between Saint-Raphaël and
Bormes-les-Mimosas. And hundreds of thousands of soldiers

disembark onto land, half of them in de Gaulle's army
and therefore counted as French even though the majority
are Algerians, Moroccans, Senegalese and Reunionese,
the colonized, in other words, not citizens of France.
This last fact plays a significant role in the history
of France and perhaps an even more significant one
in Annette's own story. But more on that later.
One last comment: many of the non-French French will die
as prisoners or will simply be murdered because to the
    Germans
they are even less French than they are to the French.

Now Marseille. On 20 and 21 August, the French
from outside and from inside, the Resistance, that is,
attack the occupying forces. A national strike
is called and an uprising declared.
The German military – their leaders – refuses
to admit defeat so soon, although or perhaps because
they've been defeated on every front. The battles
grind on. On Place Castellane, in the centre of Marseille,
near the column of Carrara marble crowned
with an allegory of the city, a stranger gives Annette
a pistol. She will use it, but won't hit anyone
or anything. First, because she accepts the necessity
of killing, but only theoretically; second,
because she doesn't know how to shoot; and third,
because there are only two bullets in the gun.
The Resistance has fewer than one thousand fighters

in this city and they are badly armed. They do know how
to aim, however, and they are determined.
The French tricolour is fluttering over the prefecture
by the twenty-first, but battles still rage. The Germans aren't
retreating, and it is only thanks to the arrival
of a general with a protracted name,
General Joseph de Goislard de Monsabert (as a point
of comparison, his German counterpart is
Lieutenant General Hans Schäfer), and especially
thanks to the arrival of the French general's
Algerian infantry troops, Moroccan goumiers and
Senegalese tirailleurs, that the occupier finally
admits defeat. With a mixture of admiration, gratitude
and an emotion she cannot name, Annette watches
impassive Berbers file past clad in finely striped djellabas,
which are not uniforms, strictly speaking, since each is
   different.
These men have come down from the High and Middle Atlas
mountains and crossed the Mediterranean to chase
the German troops from their last, ferociously defended
bastions on the hill of Notre-Dame de la Garde.
On 28 August, the enemy finally gives up.

The war has ended, at least in Toulon and in Marseille.
But peace is something else; now a war breaks out
between the French. Who collaborated or profiteered
all these years? And who risked their lives? Some
Resistance fighters have their rather peculiar methods.

Even during the Occupation collaborators were liquidated
here and there; now vengeance is extracted
with might and main. In the meantime, the rest of the
    population
feels authorized to bring supposed traitors or collaborators
to rough justice, such that cellars and garrets are again filled
with those seeking cover. Annette's life as a 'submarine'
continues, but it is nothing like life underground.
The Confederation of Youth Resistance Movements,
to which many other undercover communists belong,
elect her as its representative in the Purge Commission
of Bouches-du-Rhône. She is twenty (still only twenty!
until October) and a woman who looks much younger
than she is. She and six others, all older and all men,
are charged with a kind of cleansing that is not ethnic
like the previous one, but ethical: they must separate
the real collaborators from those merely accused of it.
In truth, the committee is there primarily to protect people
from each other, since many are taking advantage
of the widespread chaos to easily dispatch their wife's lover,
their business competitor or someone they just don't like.
During the Occupation and shortly after, nearly
eight thousand men and women are summarily
liquidated. Fewer than eight hundred are executed
after being tried in court. What Annette and her commission
are trying to contain is the *épuration sauvage*,
the so-called wild purge, which is nothing more than
whitewashed assassination and private vengeance.

75

Their task is to decide which of these pale creatures
dragged from their cellar hideouts should stand trial
and which should be released. The first difficulty lies
in distinguishing between the real and the alleged
collaborators once they've been eased from their own cellars
into that of the prefecture, where they are, for the moment,
more secure. The second difficulty: which rumours
have something to them? And what exactly counts
as collaboration? How should Annette qualify someone like
the jam manufacturer who, in order to obtain the sugar
he needed, maintained very friendly relations
with the Germans? Not particularly admirable, true,
but not criminal either. Besides, the case is not about him
but his son, who also maintained even friendlier relations
with German officers, only his was a different kind of sugar:
the dashing blonde beasts were his weakness. With women
it was called horizontal collaboration. Father and son
appear before Annette's small tribunal. The father,
who had begged and implored that his son be treated leniently,
suddenly realizes – at the same time as Annette – exactly what
his son is charged with. His head high, he stalks indignantly
out of the chamber. His son, a Nazi or collaborator, that's one
        thing,
but a poof! (Annette reads this declaration as clear as day
on Monsieur Confiture's greasy face.)

Members of the commission always work in pairs:
one plays prosecutor, the other defence. Annette

scrupulously combs through each file, calls up witnesses,
examines all the circumstances. She is all the more
    conscientious
knowing that neither her age, nor especially her sex,
are to her advantage. In the Resistance, it was the opposite.
No SS or Gestapo officer had enough imagination
to suspect that this sweet, chubby-cheeked girl was in fact
a dangerous criminal. With very few exceptions,
women in the underground were given subservient tasks
just as in life in general. It was well within Annette's rights
to be arrested and executed or deported: equality of a kind.
So here she sits, surrounded by men, working
twice as hard to compensate for certain disadvantages,
including her unimposing height of five foot two.
On 15 September, when she is not quite two weeks
in her new position, a man arrives in Marseille who not only
towers over Annette but over all the rest as well,
both literally and figuratively: it is General de Gaulle,
the general of Gaul, or France under Vercingetorix.
His name sounds made-up, but it is his actual patronymic
and his approximate rank as well. For four years,
the BBC broadcast his patriotic vibrato
for all to hear. And here is its enormous soundbox.
According to the welcoming reception plan,
the seven members of the commission wait
in a separate room of the prefecture for de Gaulle
to finish his speech and inspect the troops
before coming to survey their civilian unit.

But there are delays in de Gaulle's young Gaul.
The civilians wait. After some time, the door opens
to a crowd of men. A veritable statue of a man
towers so markedly over the rest, they seem
to be carrying him. His height of six and a half feet
is augmented by something we'll call a hat, so as not
to use the ridiculous name of kepi. Filled with expectation,
Annette studies this colossus, next to whom Raymond
    Aubrac –
who was captured by Klaus Barbie's men but then escaped,
thanks to his audacious wife Lucie – looks small,
as do the others. De Gaulle, to whom Annette had hoped
to be introduced, nods vaguely to the right and left
before disappearing on the horizon with his satellites.
From her position as 'submarine', she sees him advance
swiftly with titanic steps, towing France behind him.
Class struggle or not, she can't help but idolize
this gigantic, pious bourgeois or at least bow down
before him, secretly, of course, never admitting it
to her comrades or even, perhaps, to herself.
They are not invited to the lunch. Annette recalls:
I'd just caught a glimpse of him when he turned on his heel
in a silence so heavy, you'd have thought
we were facing a catastrophe.

Now that Annette is no longer Nobody but,
from one day to the next, officially has become Somebody,
all that belonged to her previous life returns and fills her

core: the soft, cool marine air (of that other sea, her native
    one),
the sharp peninsula of Saint-Jacut, the sweet meat
inside the scallop shell. All this and much more,
the broad expanse of her brief childhood, which endures,
like all childhoods do, even though it ended long ago
despite her meagre twenty years. Suddenly, the thought
of her family returns as well: her father Jean, Mémère and
Petite Marthe, her mother. How are they? Are they alive?
Bombs are falling on Brittany. St Malo is still embattled.
Her father lived dangerously enough before, hiding the
    children
Annette had saved. And what about Simone and Daniel,
are they still safe? For months – or was it years? – she,
being Nobody, thought of no one; now those who disappeared
reappear full force. When a man in de Gaulle's entourage
addresses her paternally, mistaking her for someone else,
she thinks of her own father. Since this man is here
and might know how, she asks him if there's a way
she could send word to her parents, give a sign of life?
He tears a page from his notebook and she scribbles
a few words – I'm fine, I'm in Marseille, how are you – words
that eventually do reach Dinan a few months later,
at a time when her family had already learned what they'd so
    longed
to know. A message from de Gaulle or, rather, from his 'house',
as his entourage is called, just as a church is called God's house
or, before the Revolution, the king's household

79

was called la Maison du Roi. For a long time, Annette has
    no word
from her parents, but after a few weeks she learns the names
of those in Dinan killed by bombs.
Her family is not among them.

While residents of Paris and Marseille are gathering
for military parades, and receptions and commissions
are busy with their purges, battles still rage across Europe.
Annette has much to do. The cellars are only slowly being
    cleared.
As essential a task as it is to sift real collaborators from the
    alleged,
the truly evil from the misguided, Annette craves a different
    kind
of engagement. To be exact, she wants to fight, yes,
to fight, here and now, before it's finally or even just tempo-
    rarily too late.
She's had it with organizing-bicycling-waiting-walking-
    hauling-sifting.
No, she wants to fight like a true combatant, weapon in hand.
True, she's not much more than five feet tall and weighs,
    let's say,
seven and a half stone, but that doesn't matter. Battles
haven't been fought with spears for ages, and how hard can it be
to use a Sten or a tommy gun? It's what she wants!
Her heart is set on it. She can't think of anything else,
especially since a new battalion of maquisards is being formed

to be deployed in Lorraine. Annette is relentless. She insists
until she is finally granted a medical examination.
After a cursory glance, the Corsican doctor with a bristling
  moustache
declares: Too puny. We can't use you. She seethes with rage.
After so many dangers, hungry days, so much trouble and
  suffering,
she's still not taken seriously and probably never will be.
Annette wants to fight, certainly, but at the same time, she
  wants to weep,
to find comfort in her parents' arms as real soldiers some-
  times do,
although they don't admit it. And she thinks again of Chen,
the communist from Shanghai in Malraux's novel,
who is ordered by some Party functionary controlled by
  Moscow
to lay down his arms. To receive this order, Chen travels
six days straight to a large city called Hankou, which is now
just a district of the much larger city Wuhan. In any case,
it never occurs to Chen to follow the functionary's orders.
He dies a death that is both unavoidable and desired but also
pointless and stupid. There is an urge in Annette, too,
to sacrifice herself and die and to defy those who want to
  prevent
her. How many die young without wanting to die? Annette
will grow old, very old indeed, with or even because of this
  urge
to dedicate her life to others or else simply to leave this life.

What she does not know (almost no one does), and this surely
would have fanned her rage, is that the brigade
she ardently wants to join will be led by Colonel Berger,
a pseudonym hiding none other than Lieutenant Colonel
    André Malraux,
who joined the Resistance just six months earlier.

I offer you my life and you don't want it? Annette does not
let herself get discouraged. When the commission is dissolved
in November '44 and the Party allows Annette to return to Paris,
she finds new grounds for hope. Couldn't the renowned
Colonel Fabien – Pierre Georges is his real name, a man who
    fought
in Spain like Malraux – couldn't he use her help? Didn't he and
Albert Ouzoulias command soldiers who were not even twenty
in the Bataillons de la jeunesse? She doesn't know, or has
    chosen
to forget, that these young fighters were all men or boys.
What she does not forget, and this both inspires and unnerves
    her,
is that most were captured in the spring of '42 and executed
at Fort Mont-Valérien or elsewhere. Roland, her beloved Roland,
is also dead. And she, too, will die. Yet, in the best case,
doesn't the human condition include the freedom to decide
    when
and for what cause to die? She wants to die as she wishes.

The Party disappoints her. Instead of offering her a chance
to sacrifice her life, it wants her to instruct the newly
    enfranchised
women voters in the ladies' magazine *Filles de France* how to cook
with next to nothing or knit a new pair of gloves from a
    moth-eaten
sweater. When Annette announces that her assignment is
    inane –
a women's magazine? Didn't we just achieve equality? –
she is declared unworthy of communism. My word.

All that was slowly accumulating inside her
and weighing on her soul, or whatever the equivalent is
for those who have no God, finally bursts. For too long,
her only companions have been fear exhaustion loneliness.
She can't go on. In Parc Monceau, instead of the calm
she's seeking, she experiences an anguish
she has never felt before. For months she has walked every inch
of this large city, she knows every district, every corner,
and yet there is no one who cares for her, not a single person
who might ask her anything at all or give her
a moment's thought, no one, nothing – emptiness.
Isn't communism about community? As long as she was
    engaged
in action she knew was meaningful (or at least hoped
was), she could cope. And now? The stately town houses
surrounding her and Parc Monceau are cloaked in silence.
The Duke of Orleans had conceived of the park

as a half-Chinese, half-English 'land of illusions',
a kind of eighteenth-century theme park with pagoda,
pyramid and ruins as authentically ruined as today's
factory-shredded jeans. Annette is not thinking of the Duke
or of us, but of her very own land of illusions,
her dream of a new communal life that had long been
her only homeland but has begun to crumble.

Every day, she spends hour after hour at the Hotel Lutetia,
recently the residence of the German military intelligence
and the SS, now a meeting place for gaunt, emaciated
    figures
freed from the camps and prisons and still barely able
to stay on their feet. Roland is dead. But how can she be sure
with such confusion? Maybe the pretty blonde was
    mistaken.
For many others, as it is for her, the Lutetia is now
the Last Hope Hotel. Under the glow of crystal chandeliers,
living skeletons stagger across a vast, opulent art deco lobby
and through a distant, inaccessible and beautiful time,
a belle époque. Many relatives come, like Annette, in vain.
They wait; day after day, they return and scrutinize
thousands of hollow-cheeked faces. Yet something
    unfathomable
lurks in the abyss of their eye sockets. Something
that has neither meaning nor name.

Pause.

Pause.

Pause.

There is a reunion, after all – just not the one Annette
had hoped for. The day after she almost collapsed
in Parc Monceau under the burden of the previous months'
exhaustion and solitude, which descended on her like the
    weight
of the park's monuments and their classical ruins,
she returns home, to Dinan. The trip is long and seems
even longer because she's heading not towards death but
backwards, in the direction of her birth. At one point
she drives through a wasteland, a landscape of ruins
that, unlike those of Parc Monceau, are not at all artificial.
She, who is anticlerical to the core and recognizes no god
as hers, looks at the stumps of church towers to the right
and left and feels, strangely, as if her own limbs
had been amputated. The villages are silent under the rain,
devastated like the factories. But the enormous granite
    viaduct
in Dinan towers unharmed. After many stops and detours,
she stands on it, looking down on her childhood
from a vertiginous height, as if from a distant star,
as if she suddenly were the elderly woman she is today.
And now comes a different kind of pause in her story,
not out of sorrow and dread this time, no, we will simply
look away as she approaches her parents' house on foot

in the dark and sees, in a lantern's cone of light, the
     silhouette
of a cyclist in plus fours and argyle knee socks,
the very clothes her father (like Tintin) often wears,
not for a round of golf but because they're practical
for riding a bicycle. Let's look away a while longer
as Annette returns after her long odyssey
to her childhood home, where no white wire fox terrier
awaits to recognize the traveller, but Mémère
and Petite Marthe wait with open arms.

Then, one day, the Germans are finally defeated.
No prospect, now, of joining the fight. The Party has turned
its focus to influence and propaganda. If she can't sacrifice
her own life, at least she can save others as always was her
     plan.
With little enthusiasm, Annette resumes her medical studies
in Rennes. She studies and learns. She learns
many things by heart, like before, but now instead
of street names schedules pseudonyms identifying marks,
she memorizes lymph nodes blood vessels nerves bones.
She feels no joy. She misses Roland. Annette gradually
becomes aware that she, herself, is absent. She is no longer
Nobody, but she also still isn't Somebody, as she'd assumed.
She feels blurred, her outline smudged. Occasionally,
she wonders with a start of fear if she is condemned to this
intermediate state, if she will always float without a firm
     foothold

or support. She easily learns the names of the minor muscles
and the smallest bones, but has no idea how to inhabit
her own body. And then a letter arrives. Robert
from Marseille. Yes, she remembers. A young man,
artistically inclined, who did not lose his softer side
in the Resistance. What does he write? Well,
that he will soon be leaving for Indochina, where
he has been posted, and also that he loves Annette and
ardently wants her to be his wife. Yes. Annette says: yes.
Love, in any case, is over. For her, that was Roland.
As for marriage, why not, if this man is as gentle and
as good as he seems... Annette senses that she needs
some kind of support, that she cannot manage alone.
Most important, however, is Indochina. There, the fight
         goes on!
Or, rather, the fight has just begun. For Annette,
it's the same fight: a country is being occupied and
oppressed but this time in France's name and therefore
in hers. The same general who, on de Gaulle's orders,
resisted the Germans with such courage – Jean
de Lattre de Tassigny, another protracted name –
the same one who, or more accurately whose African soldiers,
liberated Marseille and Toulon, is now fighting
the Vietnamese led by Ho Chi Minh.
These generals seem to find occupation
of foreign countries legitimate, as long as they
are the occupiers. It takes Annette a few days
to get to Marseille and a few weeks to become a wife.

It takes her a few months to get divorced. Divorce is always
a tiresome, drawn-out affair. Marriage, Indochina,
the good fight: farewell! How could this be?
What happened is that Robert's position in Indochina
was a government post. And the government,
which was fighting the communists in Asia, was not about
to import a communist, even one of their own.
So, Robert lost both wife and job. After a few weeks of
    marriage,
Annette could no longer bear life with him, gentle as he
    was.
What had drawn her, after all, wasn't his temperament
but the Viet Minh's aggressive tactics. What was she to do
with a husband who was not Roland and not even
a militant communist?

Because of her flash marriage, she's back in Marseille.
She hasn't left the Party's utopia yet, but she rubs against
its borders and its limits now and then. One not so fine day,
    for example,
a Communist Party functionary, a man aware of her
    underground
and 'submarine' past, taps her to infiltrate and spy on the B
    family.
Why them? Because they are accused of being different.
It's serious: the father has a beard and smokes cigars
from Havana, where the regime at the moment is nowhere near
communist. The Bs are Poupou – what kind of a name

88

is that for a man in his fifties? – and Clicli – another
    ridiculous
name, this one for a woman always elegantly coiffed
and manicured. And how is it that they live in a villa?
They're generous to a fault, it's true. But still,
where did they get their wealth? What kind of
communists do they think they are, these people?
The father, Poupou, and one of his adult sons
are in the banana business. Could be worse. But
he sells his bananas to the Germans! If that's not
    suspicious…
Annette can't help it, she likes them. Didn't they
find her a room when she was on the street? And now
she's supposed to snoop on them? She thinks of her father,
Jean, who often said that one half of the communists
were always busy spying on the other. And now they
expect her to join the spying half? She remembers
a few people she spied on in the past, but
they weren't communists. She'd somewhat recognized
the necessity of surveillance back then, even if
she wasn't proud of taking part. But this lovely family?
Annette, finally twenty-one, harbours several souls
or people, as so many of us do, although two
of these are quite distinct: there is one Annette, daughter
of Jean and Petite Marthe, who knows without thinking
what to do in certain situations that require difficult
decisions. She knows what is right and what is not
through some instinct, inherited or taught. The other

89

Annette, the second one, is first and foremost
communist. This Annette also doesn't need to think,
although instead of listening to her own conscience,
she listens to the Party. She does what she was taught
to do in the Resistance because it was imperative,
a matter of life and death: she obeys. She does so
all the more submissively, since she still feels
hollowed out; essentially she's still Nobody.
She has lost her footing and that's exactly what
the Party offers her with its promises of solidarity
and a shining future. And so, when it comes to spying
on the Bs, the second Annette wins the upper hand
despite the first Annette's objections. She will do it, yes,
she will spy on her comrades. She has qualms, but
the banana business seems suspect, doesn't it?
The war is over, to be sure, but certain fronts remain:
Germany may no longer be Nazi, but it is imperialist
and under America's sway. Ergo, someone doing business
with the Germans is no longer seen as collaborating
with Fascists but with German capitalists, not much better
from the Party's point of view. So then:

In order to gain access to the Bs' home and find out more
about them, Annette seduces Pierre, one of the two sons.
She finds this project of seduction repugnant, but perhaps
there's more than a little temptation in playing Mata Hari
for a time. Once she has penetrated the lion's den,
she realizes it's far more fun inside than out.

The elegant mother Clicli likes to belt out arias
from *La Traviata* to Pierre's exuberant accompaniment
on the piano, while his brother Claude teaches Annette
the most effective judo throws, which may come in handy
someday. Claude's young son also likes to sing and squeaks
ear-piercing arias. Is this what traitors look like these days?
Little by little, she learns more: Poupou, once a poor
    coalman,
left his hometown in Auvergne on foot in search of a future
that, if not brilliant, would at least not be coal-black.
He made it to Paris and then to London, where he met
    Clicli
after getting to know her brother in a pub, that is. From
    then on
his future was named Clicli, as well as banana. What else
is there to add? At once conscientiously and half-heartedly,
Annette delves into the Bs' import–export business
without uncovering anything other than a happy family.
The Party cadre won't ease up: these people are traitors,
class enemies! After a while, Annette can no longer bear
the dishonesty and deceit. She confesses all to Poupou.
The shame of it! She weeps. Poupou relights his cigar.
Yes, well, he says. And he consoles her. He's seen worse.
He shipped arms during the Spanish Civil War. Told the Party
to go to hell in '39 when their Soviet big brother
made a pact with the Devil. Remained a communist
but with no support other than his own heart and
a few pamphlets. So then. They want to knock him off.

He sits across from Annette, breathing so deeply
his shoulders seem to swell.

Another lesson learned. Shame is a good teacher.
One of the best. More disillusions follow, one
after another. Annette understood well before
Khrushchev's report in '56. And yet the cup of shame
and indignation has yet to overflow. For later inhabitants
of this earth, of which Annette herself is one, it's hard
to understand how this *ism*, governed by Moscow and
managed by the Party, could have become a creed,
a new faith, especially for those who, like herself,
have no sense or taste for religion, that opium of the masses.
But that is how it is or was: for her, no other word
captures this kind of submission and blind obedience
to a higher power than faith. It's the same as with a great love,
which renders the lover blind to blemishes or flaws
that are perfectly obvious to everyone else. How much
more real the people, places and systems
of our dreams are than any reality!

At twenty-three, Annette marries a second time, and
successfully. Not only is Joe – Joseph Roger – a
communist, but as Commandant Darcourt, he liberated
Paris in August '44. Not alone, of course. With his men,
many of whom perished, he pushed nearly five hundred
    German
soldiers into the Prince Eugène barracks on

Place de la République and trapped them there. A communist
and former resistance fighter, then, but also – again,
like Annette – a doctor. The conditions are promising,
even excellent if marriage is considered not, or not merely,
as a passion but as a union of two people who
understand each other well. Furthermore,
she's pregnant. Joe is a friend, comrade, lover, hero.
What more could one want? A real husband?
He can fill that role too.

From this point on, they will lose their illusions
together. Is that a consolation? We're talking of
illusions about humanity, not marriage. They'll share
their disenchantment with countless others. Some
have a head start in abandoning their illusions, others
lag behind. Annette and Joe, in the middle of the peloton,
leave the Party in 1956. But before then they engage in
a number of activities, primarily political: debates, travel,
Warsaw, Leipzig, four months in Moscow studying
the importance of sleep for memory. She is under
constant surveillance. The Party parades her here
and there to lull her into complacency,
but she is more refractory and clear-sighted than
these flunkeys realize. Back in France, she and Joe
become dissidents.

Joe and Annette's love, in equal parts a friendship,
is inextricably entwined with another history, that

of the Communist Party. Together they want to believe,
together they lose faith. Is that the beginning
of the end? Once they've lost faith in the Party,
their belief in conjugal love begins to wane.

During this time, Annette becomes a neurophysiologist
and the mother of two sons. She works in a clinic in
Marseille, but spends much time elsewhere and
occupied with other things. Talking, debating, that's all fine,
but for her, politics is action. It's just as well, since
in the fifties, thinking is reserved for men. You can
be a doctor and do complicated research, but when
it comes to meeting other dissidents, the men drone on and on
while the women sit in the next room folding flyers
by the hundreds and addressing envelopes. Annette's
lively mind and agile tongue demand activity; theory
only gains meaning through action. Talking or
thinking without acting is as foreign to her as
constant prayer without any effort to provide for
or help those in need would be to a devout Christian.
Speaking of providing and helping: in Annette both
are instincts or reflexes rather than commandments,
a behaviour, in any case, that requires no thought or
calculation, such that – just don't tell her! – without
wanting to be or even knowing she is, Annette is a truer
Christian than many believers are. On this point,
less a point, actually, than a broad expanse of generosity
and helpfulness, we'll have more to say.

Since her marriage, her life is both very different and exactly the same. She's no longer alone and is no longer poor – that makes an enormous difference. Her
   circumstances
are bourgeois, sometimes that just happens. You briefly look away and the next thing you know, you're *Doctor, sir* or *Doctor, ma'am*; their apartment is so large, Annette almost gets lost in it. The building once belonged to Napoleon's
   sister,
rumour has it, and now her in-laws own it. Joe's father, one of the most respected doctors in Marseille, has a soft spot for his new daughter-in-law. In what respect is Annette's life the same as it was before? Inasmuch as she still treats everyone the same, not in terms of friendship, it's true, but in terms of the equal respect she accords to all, whatever their position or social rank. Chief physicians, nurses, her in-laws and the couple that lives with them and looks after their children, Annette sees them all in the same light.

Her life is also the same inasmuch as her door is always open to those who need a place to stay or a bite to eat. Her tone of voice, her manners are simple and straightforward, no doubt due to Mémère, who is always with Annette, looking over her shoulder, even if no longer physically there.

Soon another is physically absent, yet always present.
Her father, Jean, dies and leaves Petite Marthe alone
with their bistro in Dinan. Annette occasionally visits
her mother in her beloved Brittany. And so it is
that one Saturday afternoon, as she's driving along
a lonely road, she passes a couple whose car
has broken down. Annette would not be Annette
if she failed to stop and ask if she could help, and
she can. On Saturday afternoons, all garages
are closed, so the two need a place to stay.
Annette is ready to find them one. It's quite simple:
when you know Annette, you also know how
to find lodgings. She is about to bring the couple,
two Germans, home with her, when she hears the husband
speaking excitedly and proudly to his wife while pointing
out of the window at a spot he seems to recognize.
Annette looks at him; he repeats himself but this time
in English, a language she understands well enough
to catch that over there, next to that barn, he'd arrested
two people during the war. Annette slams on the brakes
and throws them out. What an idiot! Those he arrested
had to be from the Resistance and might easily
have been her or her friend Roland. She drives on a few
hundred metres, then turns around and picks up
the two Germans she had left on the side of the road.
She doesn't say a word to her passengers and drops
them off in front of the hotel. Let them fend
for themselves! To this day, the couple probably

has no idea why the young Frenchwoman reacted
so strangely. Those who need an explanation
for certain things will never understand. Not worth
the trouble. She gives up.

Annette's new life is pleasant. Her children
are her heart's delight and her husband, if not ideal,
is more than fine, her marriage, too, for that matter,
with the usual highs and lows. Her work interests her,
although it's not her dream job, but then what is?
Adventurer, insurgent, Robin Hood? The only careers
that come to mind are men's work and not even, strictly
    speaking,
real professions. In the mid-1950s, Annette is in her thirties
and has been leading a life of a Somebody for some time.
She'd be happy enough to keep living it
indefinitely, at least so long as nothing came to
interrupt its course. Does she wish it would? We don't know;
nor does she. Maybe it's the opposite: marriage
and family life, her work as a doctor, create a joyful
whole that offers her warmth and fulfilment. She
is doing very well. The incidents that take place
and will be recorded in history books as the 'events'
intrude most inopportunely and trouble her domestic
and professional happiness. These things do happen.
We don't know the whole truth but have reason to believe
that the truth contains several contradictions and has
at least two versions.

Which 'events' are these? Four decades later,
in 1999, they are given an official name: war.
Until then people speak of events, more precisely
of Algerian events, which is rather odd because the events
extend across all of France and because Algeria
is not a 'colony' or a 'protectorate' but is a part
of France, consisting of three *départements*, no less
départements than, say, Bouches-du-Rhône, Gard
and Seine-Maritime are. (We are talking about
the small part of Algeria that is not desert; the desert
is French, too, but is under the army's control.) This
is the situation in '54, and that's where the 'events' start.
The inhabitants of these three *départements* – the majority,
about nine out of ten – begin to ask, and not without cause,
why they live in France if they're not French. In Algeria,
of course, the 'French' are the real French, that is,
those who emigrated to Algeria from France, but also
those whose ancestors came from other European countries
and settled there. The non-French, most of them
    disenfranchised,
are all the rest, the so-called indigenous people, or *indigènes*.
    Basically,
nine-tenths of the Algerians are asking the very same
    question
Emmanuel-Joseph Sieyès asked in 1789 in the name of
more than nine-tenths of the French: What is the Third
    Estate?

Everything. What has it been hitherto in the political order?
Nothing. What does it desire to be? To be something…
That sums it up. Robbed of all the fertile farmland
and without work – there's no industry to speak of here –
these French non-French live in crowded slums,
like the shanty towns of Nanterre, called *bidonvilles*,
which are closer to *favelas* than to *banlieues*. The homes there
aren't built of stone; they're low shacks of corrugated metal,
roofing paper and wood. Diseases are rampant
and children are constantly dying and being born,
whereas in the city centres of Algiers and Oran
the elegant French go to the cinema, drive fast cars
and lounge on café terraces with milky-yellow
anise-flavoured drinks, pretending they're in some
European capital. Since 1830, the French nation
has prided itself on its civilizing mission
in Algeria (*bonjour*, Tocqueville). Indeed,
one hundred years later France has managed to teach
six per cent of men and two per cent of women to read and
write.
They could have done better, one would think, perhaps
by applying the principles on which they pride themselves:
liberté, égalité, fraternité…

Back to 1954. The Indochina War has just ended
with France one colony smaller (without Annette's
assistance), and 'events' break out elsewhere. In truth,
they started much earlier, in '45 in Sétif and in Kabylia,

a demonstration, an uprising, thousands dead,
one hundred of whom are French. Everything
always starts much earlier. The Algerian tirailleurs,
those Algerian soldiers who fought in 1944 and often
died in battle – the same ones Annette saw marching
into Marseille – were conscripted into military service
even though they weren't French citizens.
They had to serve two years, not ten months
like the French, and they were given lower pay.
Looking further back, it's even worse:
the Popular Front was unable to improve
their situation in '36, and in '54 Pierre Mendès France
and François Mitterand, respectively Minister
of Foreign Affairs and Minister of the Interior, were
anything but advocates of an independent Algeria.

In the summer of that year, Annette travels to Algeria,
not to fight but on holiday, to visit friends.
We're relieved to note that she is not entirely
opposed to rest and relaxation in the summer.
The events, the initial ones, occur
a few months later, on All Saints' Day. (Nine-tenths
of the population is Muslim but the holidays
are Catholic – does that add fuel to the fire?)
Annette has been invited to visit friends who run
an orange and geranium farm in southern Algeria.
Sometimes ascent can be swift: Annette's grandmother,
Mémère, was as poor as the workers on this farm,

but at least she didn't have a foreman. Her granddaughter
has made a leap into a different world. As a doctor
she frequents other doctors, lawyers, professors and
progressive farm owners. The farm owners, her friends,
are *Pieds-Noirs*, as people of European origin
living in Algeria are rather puzzlingly called,
and they speak of those born here as of brothers who need
only a bit more schooling to be their equals and no longer
subservient, but at the same time, they employ foremen and
overseers who are most assuredly not brothers
to the workers. Annette's friends have no presentiment
of the events that she senses in the air, yet the air
is so heavy with scents of geranium, fig and
orange blossom that it masks the smell of budding
rebellion for those who would rather not
perceive it. And can we know how much
time misery humiliation oppression it takes
for people to decide they've had enough?
In the Shanghai of Malraux's *Man's Fate*
there's a Belgian worker named Hemmelrich,
who can only bring himself to revolt, to put his life
on the line after his wife and young son are butchered
by counter-revolutionaries. Cowardice
is not the only thing that can trap you
in apathy – not only in a novel but in real life too.

On the other side of the Mediterranean, Annette
is ashamed to be one of the whites, the *petits blancs* or

colons, who are generally unpopular, if not despised.
She isn't used to being one of the dominant
or powerful in any land, much less her own,
and she's not about to adapt now. She watches
the waiters in the Hotel Transatlantic pouring
the guests tea as if giving them poison. She
never liked being served – there are people like that,
who prefer to do everything themselves, which is
complicated in hotels and restaurants – but here
it's something else. Here she has the sense
that the staff hate her, not her personally, but
her as a Frenchwoman, the embodiment of
the injustice they suffer every day. She finds it
hard to bear and returns to Marseille with the distinct
impression that Algeria is seething and France
will soon again be one colony smaller.

After this trip, as once before, Annette begins
to slip, slowly and imperceptibly, into a kind
of resistance movement, this time not against
a foreign invader but against her own country
and her government, against herself, so to speak.
In 1954, she is still a member of the Communist Party.
They're not particularly interested in the Algerians'
independence movements (granted, a bit more
than any other political party, but still). Their
rallying cry, after all, is *workers of the world,
unite*, not separate into new nationalities.

We are one giant nation of the oppressed,
we don't need another: that, more or less,
is their motto, with which Annette and others
increasingly disagree. That she encourages the few
Algerian women who timidly attend the meetings
to speak is acceptable, if naive; but when she
brings up the Algerian farmers and fellahs
as if it were the Party's duty to defend them
like the workers in the factories of Renault or
the Total and Shell refineries outside Marseille,
she is reprimanded.

Soon in Algeria, therefore in France, bombs
start to explode and fires are set. In some areas,
the fellahs attack the colonial rulers with clubs
and axes. The events begin and do not stop.
The Communist Party, that is, the Algerian
Communist Party – there is only one country
but two communist parties – is outlawed
because it opposes colonialism and has allied itself
with the FLN, the separatist National Liberation
Front. Their French sibling party dithers, then
in March '56, votes to approve a decree
issued by Guy Mollet's government that places
Algeria under the French military's rule.

What kind of communists are these? Annette
has seen enough. She doesn't need Hungary on top

of this to know her mind. But what should she do?
She watches developments from a distance.
Algeria isn't far, separated from Marseille
only by a sea, crossed by ever more conscripts,
just soldiers, poor devils, not colonial masters.
With some luck and, even better, connections,
one can end up in the administration. Without them
it's necessary to do or at least witness things
one would rather not do or see, offences recounted
by the victims soon enough. The army is no longer
accountable to the parliament and does what it
deems right: torture. It believes it can crush
the insurrection this way. Annette reads about this
in the newspapers and cannot accept
that people are brutalized in her country's name,
therefore in hers as well, simply because they
want their own country back. And are tortured
to betray others. She is outraged and cannot
understand. But what spurs her to action is
a sentence in *Against Torture*, a 1957 book
by the Catholic writer Pierre-Henri Simon
(in this period, Annette has reconciled herself
with the Catholics, since they and a few dissidents
from the Communist Party are the only ones
willing to help the Algerians). In his book,
Simon says that if the French allow, without protest,
torture, humiliation and oppression to be practised
by them or in their name, then they will have been

defeated by Hitler after all. Did she risk her neck
for this country for it to employ, twenty years later,
some of the same methods as the SS? Bitterness
and rage. Her husband Joe agrees, but he is less
hot-headed and more clear-sighted (two traits
that often go together). He worries that sooner or later
in this battle for the right to vote, religion
will come to the fore, the kind of religion that is
centred on power rather than belief. Annette
ignores his words of warning. She has gradually
begun to believe that religion has its good sides,
especially when she thinks of those *prêtres ouvriers*,
worker-priests whom she occasionally meets
at demonstrations and who work in factories,
as the French Maoists would years later.
Had someone told her earlier that she'd find her way
to a new kind of resistance through a priest…
As earlier, the first step is a small one: delivering
an envelope here and there, just like before,
but this time each contains a few banknotes. It's a way to
support the families of Algerians who have been
arrested. Then comes the next step.

And years or decades later it is clear that not one
of the small gestures she made was inconsequential.
Each one proved significant, imperceptibly leading her
out of her rather quiet life as a mother and doctor
to one she neither explicitly wanted nor chose, but

at some point became her own and could no longer
be exchanged for the earlier one. In retrospect, she realizes
she'd had a choice, a choice she could not see when
she was facing the future in its inevitable uncertainty.
As long as we're moving forward, we may think
we can see, but we are in the dark. Nevertheless,
we take one small but momentous step after another
because we cannot stand still, we must keep moving.
In the end, she will have lost much of what was most
important to her. You can't have it all, we're told.
But you can have nothing. Ideal, dream, longed-for
future land, where are you? Do you still exist?
– Here! I'm here! a small voice answers faithfully
like an eternal flame, flickering unseen in the distance.

The historian Michelet wrote that although every state
in antiquity spoke of fraternity, the word applied
only to citizens, to men; the slave was but a thing.
Writing in the Antilles in 1950, Aimé Césaire
claimed that what this very distinguished, Christian
and humanist twentieth-century bourgeois never forgave
        Hitler for
was not his crimes against humanity themselves, but his
extension of treatment to white Europeans that had
        hitherto
been reserved for Blacks, Arabs and indentured Indians.
Whether or not this is true is a matter for debate.
In any case, as late as 2005 the French were debating

whether France's presence abroad played a positive role.
A law was passed – and repealed one year later – making it
compulsory to teach children the advantages of
colonization. (Voices echo from across the Rhine: after all,
Hitler built the autobahns and created lots of jobs.)
'All human beings are born free and equal in dignity and
    rights':
that's a French invention, isn't it? Among the children
who learn this fundamental principle in school, there are
some Algerian boys and girls who, at some point,
ask themselves what kind of principle it can be, if
the country prides itself on it but doesn't remotely
observe it. In this respect, if colonization
has one advantage it's that it provides grounds
for its own eradication. End of digression.

Again Annette takes up a kind of resistance to
the ruling power, but this time her country isn't occupied,
it is the occupier – and has been for a long time.
The French have been in Algeria since 1830, true,
but that was never yet a source of strife, at least not
for anyone French. It took a rebellion by the indigenous
    inhabitants
to spark those tensions. Annette joins a French group
providing assistance to the FLN. Signing petitions
was never her thing; others – Sartre Beauvoir Breton
Sarraute Duras Blanchot Truffaut, etc. – all those stars
and talking heads, although by the time they finally

manage to sign something in 1960, Annette has long
  been...
But let's not get ahead of ourselves or we'll lose all suspense.
And speaking of suspense, would it be fair to say that
it's also a spur for Annette? Certainly not her only
motivation, but a factor nonetheless? The way France
governs Algeria horrifies her, that is clear and
reason enough. But are there other reasons too?
Reasons she may not be aware of? No, everything's fine,
  thanks:
children, husband, work. Granted, her husband cheats on her
from time to time; but in such cases a simple separation
is an option – besides, they've always patched things up
before. Almost everything is fine and yet...
to act again and not just talk, to be part of an invisible,
determined group again, striving for a larger and just goal,
to go underground again, face danger and dissemble.
To play for the highest stakes once more and embrace fear,
courage, luck – in short, to *live* again. She is thirty-five.
Everything else is mere hypothesis.

In 1958, the 'events' are in their fourth year and
because the situation doesn't get better, they call in
a great man who saved France and French Algeria
from catastrophe once before, General de Gaulle.
In Algeria, he raises his long arms in the air
like the corkscrew that bears his name. For the time being,
he pulls neither corks nor teeth but from the balcony

of the General Government calls out his famous
and famously incomprehensible phrase: *Je vous ai
compris!* I have understood you. Good to know.
But whom exactly has he understood?
Less easily misunderstood is the second, no less
legendary phrase he delivers two days later:
Vive l'Algérie française! Annette doesn't wait
for de Gaulle's third declaration. She takes
her next step, which will lead her to a small group
in France, later called 'the suitcase carriers' or
the Jeanson network. Their suitcases are filled with money,
bundles of banknotes, a kind of revolution tax levied by
     the FLN
for its fight against the State and the occupiers in general.
This tax is collected from Algerians by Algerians, and
to ensure the money gets safely to Paris and then abroad,
Annette and other French activists ferry it
in their bags. These bags hold the millions of francs
the FLN needs to strengthen and expand its military
structures. Among so much in this context that Annette
and most others aren't aware of at the time is that
these millions are deposited in Switzerland,
in the Arab Commercial Bank founded and directed by
the Nazi benefactor, publisher of Goebbels' diaries and
admirer of Hitler, François Genoud. What is
his motivation for helping Muslims too? Quite simply,
his hatred of the Jews. Does the FLN put these millions
solely to good use? Certainly not. And is their goal

of independence, the focus of all their efforts, still
a just cause if they must break laws to achieve it?
Yes. Is it worth sacrificing one's life for? Again Annette
says yes. Still, that answer requires her to close
her eyes, or at least the eye that would have seen children
torn to shreds by bombs set in trams and cafés
in Algiers. Is there a more peaceful path
to independence? Is France making any attempt,
however slight, to consider the Algerians' legitimate
claims? Not at all. France opens a few more schools and grants
a few more Algerians the right to vote (the vast
majority is still disenfranchised), and that's it.
Entreaties and petitions have gone nowhere. Annette
keeps schlepping her suitcases filled with wages for
the members of the FLN and the Jeanson network.
She herself has declined any payment. She's on leave
from the clinic in Marseille, but her husband's salary
as a doctor is enough for two and he supports
her engagement. Annette covers many miles: the bags
must first be brought from the provinces to Paris
and from there to Switzerland. During this time,
her young sons are taken care of by Élise and Lucien,
friends who live with Annette and Joe and occasionally
harbour members of the FLN. But back to the suitcases:
the contributions are compulsory for the Algerians
in Algeria and those in France, which they call the
metropolis or the *mère patrie*, the mother fatherland,
as if France were not only a strict but just father

yet also a gentle, caring mother to these people
it treats as nothing more than factory hands
and cannon fodder. From the miner who descends
each day into a coal pit in Lorraine, Peugeot factory
workers or merchants of Oran to the nomads
of Algeria's high plateaus, all who consider themselves
patriots – and everyone else as well – must contribute
to the cost of this uprising or war. Those who refuse
to pay or prefer to donate funds to the wrong group –
the more moderate organization, the Algerian
National Movement (MNA), still exists and, of course,
also needs to survive and above all to fight –
risk reprisals, even death. Large amounts of money
are in play, as are the positions of power in a future
independent Algeria. That's how things are.
Could they be different? *The revolution
devours its children* is a famous adage
proclaimed by the Girondin Vergniaud in 1793
and taken up forty years later by Georg Büchner
in his play *Danton's Death*. And what did Vergniaud say
just before the adage? That we have seen a strange system
of liberty develop in which we are told: you are free
to think as you wish as long as you think as we do,
or we will denounce you to the vengeance of
the people. True, like Saturn, the revolution
will devour its children, but unlike Saturn won't
spit them out alive again years later. Instead,
it devours ever more, its children's children and

their children as well. These victims aren't real enemies,
but rivals or simply passers-by. Montagnards against
Girondins, the FLN against the MNA, bloody fratricidal
wars, death, death and more death. In the eight years
of the war, the FLN kills around nineteen thousand
    civilians,
sixteen thousand of them Algerian. Anyone caught
drinking has to pay up, fines equal to one or two
months' salary, witnesses report. The FLN wants
independence, that we know, but socialism and Islam too,
which not everyone realizes at first. Why do you
support them, Annette? Why are you risking your life
to help these people? Not for these people, you'll say,
but for all people, for humankind, for the principles
of equality and justice, for a higher end. Annette!
This end is a beautiful chimera and does not justify
the means. What do you want, she might reply,
it's war. Revolution is a monster, a powerful machine
that can't be stopped, a twenty-ton thresher forging
straight ahead, and whoever doesn't jump out of its way,
    well…
She also doesn't know what we have learned since that
    time,
as has she: the dead will not be counted until much later.
Annette only knows that some things are going awry, but
isn't that inevitable? She knows where it's all meant
to lead – to an independent nation – and for that
she needs no compass or counsel along the way.

There are always those who branch off the path or
get in the way of others. She accepts this. The journey
is long, the goal still far. She carries the suitcases,
brings them to a certain kitchen in the Parisian suburb
    Suresnes
that serves as a bank for a country that doesn't yet exist.
Here, in the home of the actor Jacques Rispal and his wife,
Yvonne, the Algerians' savings pile up. Once
Annette falls for a con man's line and by the time
she catches on, he and the suitcase are long gone.
Swindlers come with the territory, moths to the flame.
Like Annette, Rispal was in the Resistance and both
helped Jews; now they're helping Muslims. In their
eyes, it's all of a piece. Naturally, they see the differences
between the two movements, but they prefer to focus on
the similarities. They believe helping the FLN is their duty
and obligation. Conveying cash is the least they can do.

Before long, Annette will take a bigger step.
Francis Jeanson's group is too undisciplined for her.
Having absorbed the instincts and precautions
of operating underground in the Resistance,
she doesn't like their nonchalance. But there's more.
What they're doing is right, that is clear, and Jeanson
is a nice guy, but does he really need a Mercedes
as an official car? And other small things, probably
unimportant, but still, the way he waves francs
at the cleaning lady from the couch when he wants her

to buy him a bottle of Scotch. Nothing serious
or even unusual, but Annette has no patience
for this kind of thing. No matter. There are principles
and grand ideas on the one hand and what one does
and who one is on the other. Ideally, they coincide,
but in real life, they rarely, if ever, do.
Perhaps Annette expects too much.

Besides, she wonders why she should work only with
French people if the idea is to help Algerians who
want France to leave them alone. She lets herself
be recruited by a man from the FLN and is assigned
a role as an assistant or courier for Georges, whose
real name is Mohammed, she will later learn, a
supervisor of the region of southern France, or
wilaya sud. (A *wilaya* is a district or province
in Algeria, and by dividing France into their own
administrative units, the FLN exacts a kind of revenge
or equalization, almost as if the Algerian nation
that doesn't yet exist had annexed the French regions
in the same way France had divided Algeria into French
départements.) Annette's role is one she knows well
from her years in the Resistance. She organizes many
and varied accommodations and hiding places.
The FLN supervisor for whom she works
has to sleep in a different place every night; other
militants need to go undercover or meet in secret
in secure locations. Before long, Annette is weighed down

by bunches of keys like the caretaker of some large school.
Through friends, colleagues and former comrades,
she has access to an array of second homes, beach huts
and caravans. The risk is minimal. After all, the owners
can plead ignorance of how their friend, a decent person, a
 doctor,
a Frenchwoman, no less, wanted to use their second homes,
but the risk is there. Even if Algeria is not a cause
many would risk their necks for, the heavy key rings show
that in certain circles there is a great deal of solidarity. Later,
when the Jeanson network is put on trial, Sartre will
 proclaim
that he would have put up anyone from the FLN, if only
he'd been asked. In fact, supporting the group in writing
can also cost you your life. Annette's role is to drive
Georges and other members of the FLN here and there.
That's all? You wouldn't think that driving people
around and putting them up for the night could
entail much risk. But you'd be wrong, since these
people are considered terrorists.

The French Republic is now governed by the nation's
saviour, de Gaulle. Under his administration
there is no less torture than there had been before.
André Malraux, the hero of Annette's childhood and
creator of the young terrorist Chen, is named Minister
in 1958. First, he is put in charge of the Ministry of
Information, then moved to a cabinet created

especially for him, the Ministry of Culture, where
he can amuse himself without creating difficulties
for the policymakers. He announces that de Gaulle
will put an end to torture, yet it is still practised
not only in Algeria, where it's the army's remit and
no one sees it, but also in French police stations
and the domestic intelligence agency, the DST,
at 11, Rue des Saussaies, the building that housed
the Gestapo's headquarters fifteen years before.

If a nation employs the same methods as the Gestapo,
it doesn't matter how many Malrauxes it has as
ministers. Annette does not believe she owes it
obedience. In disobeying, she follows
the commands of her conscience, which leads
her in 1959 along many rural roads in
southern France. Unlike in the Resistance,
there's now always someone with her,
a passenger who talks to her about the FLN's origins
and aims along with many other topics. As long
as she and Georges are driving in the car
they are reasonably safe, but as soon as they
get out, which, of course, they can't avoid,
they are at risk. This leads Annette to adopt
yet another role alongside courier, chauffeur
and right hand, that of sociologist of style.
Mustering all her powers of persuasion, she tries
to dissuade the men of the FLN, many of whom

are newly arrived in France, from dressing like
pimps, their hair slicked back, feet in patent leather shoes
and torsos squeezed into shiny rayon jackets.
They left their wardrobes on the other side of
the Mediterranean and believe their new look will
make them pass for French, when instead
it makes them easy targets for the police. Annette
transforms those who are willing into inconspicuous
Everymen. One day, she has a similar problem
with her boss, Georges. She has to accompany him
to St-Tropez, where all of Paris, i.e. Sartre and
Brigitte Bardot, can be found. At the very least, Georges
needs new trousers and a sleeveless T-shirt, which
is all the rage. After much cajoling, he agrees
to wear it under his shirt, and given the extremely
unfashionable pallor of his arms from which dangle
his suspiciously dark hands, his reservations are
well founded. Often in retrospect, Annette's adventures
sound comical and perhaps there was an element of play
and innocence to that time, if that is possible in such
contexts. They don't think at every moment
of the very real dangers they are running, for example,
there in St-Tropez. (Incidentally, whose bright idea
was it to set up a meeting in the very place where the most
photographers, policemen and journalists are concentrated,
where all the eyes of France are directed?) And yet
perhaps they were safest there, since it would never occur
to anyone that a fugitive would want to hide here,

right in the lion's den, where everyone else
is on conspicuous display. In fact, all goes well.

(Georges not only thinks the clothes he's meant to wear
ridiculous, but also, Annette is pleased to hear,
much too expensive.)

On 16 September 1959, history swerves. After
one hundred and thirty years of occupation and five years
of war, Charles de Gaulle announces over the radio and
television waves that the time has come to ask the
    Algerians
if they would rather govern themselves or continue
to be ruled by France. The *Pieds-Noirs*, the French in
    Algeria,
fulminate: isn't it clear what the answer will be, when
nine-tenths of the population are asked if they want
the remaining tenth to keep control over them?
Why bother asking? But let's not jump the gun. We're
not even close to that stage yet. The referendum on
self-determination will not be held until
the Algerians put down their arms and make peace,
more precisely, at the most four years after
peace is made. And the threshold for peace,
according to de Gaulle, will be reached when
there are no more than two hundred casualties
from attacks and ambushes a year. A distant
reality, in other words, but it is the first time that

someone in the upper echelons has ever said anything
about self-determination. At the same time de Gaulle,
or rather his troops under General Challe, are fighting
a fiercer war than ever before in order to secure themselves
a strong negotiating position when independence
looms – as it inevitably will. At stake
are nuclear weapon tests and the oil in the Sahara.
In this year, hundreds of thousands of Algerians,
families, children, entire villages are displaced
from their land and interned in camps. They are
also – and this is the point – cut off from the partisans.
At the same time that de Gaulle is speaking of peace
and self-determination, hundreds are dying of hunger
every day. It sounds cynical, and it is,
but it's also progress.

As they drive through the country, Annette and Georges
talk about this situation and much more. She trusts him
and the FLN, at least the only side she knows, which is
the French arm of the movement. Algeria, despite it all,
has set up a provisional government, based in Tunis,
just as Charles de Gaulle's government-in-exile
had been based in London. This gives rise to many
bitter arguments and debates in France, which Annette
finds rather surprising since mute obedience
was the rule in her time with the Resistance. She concludes
that this still non-existent state will be completely democratic.
Other developments lead her to believe it will also be

a modern and revolutionary state. In the meantime,
she must drive. Georges, as usual, is her passenger.
They're making their way along a steep back road
that is full of potholes and almost too tight
for their vehicle and not in a metaphorical sense.
There are so many potholes that a man as tall
as Georges can't help but bump his head. He hunches
in his seat, humming absent-mindedly. Suddenly
he realizes that it's a song he was forced to sing
at school in Constantine, standing at attention
before the blue, white and red flag of France:
Maréchal, nous voilà! Here we are, Marshal Pétain,
France's saviour, and so on. The things they forced
into his head! Luckily Annette and her car are here
to shake it all loose.

Among the other FLNers she has to chauffeur
here and there, there's one whose code name is Paul
(his real name is Younsi). She suspects him at first sight.
Early on in her time underground with the Resistance,
Annette developed a sixth sense that told her
who was trustworthy and, above all, who was not.
She does not trust Paul. She observes him with a doctor's cold,
clinical gaze and it's clear to her that this is someone
whose problems could quickly become a danger
for her. She remembers several situations in Arles,
in Avignon, in Nîmes, when Paul behaved peculiarly.
She tries to draw Georges' attention to Paul's oddities,

but he won't listen to a word she says.
He even reacts angrily, his anger spurred, perhaps,
by his own doubts as to Paul's reliability. And so
things take their course as they are wont to do.
In hindsight, this course replays endlessly in slow motion
and certain details loom large. Rather than mere details,
they now seem to be the hand of fate, which uses a Paul
or a Mark or a Matthew for its ends. This hand is shrewd
and has many tricks, as does Annette, and she could have
slipped through its fingers if she'd been a bit more
circumspect; in other words, if she hadn't been Annette.

As instructed, she drives Younsi, alias Paul, to Alès
outside Montpellier. The road is winding and, to Paul's
barely concealed worry, Annette must stop the car
two or three times because of nausea. Paul seems less
    concerned
about her health than some arrangement that will
fall through if she has to turn back. He's relieved to learn
that Annette is merely suffering a bout of morning sickness.
She wants to drop him off and leave right away, as planned,
but she has to wait a long time for him in an isolated house
with a family that is ostensibly his. He finally returns
and gives her a letter she is to deliver into Georges' hands
that very evening. Paul tries, as he often has before,
to find out from Annette exactly what route she will take
when she drives Georges back to Paris the next day.
She pretends the route has not yet been decided.

Once again, Annette wonders if Younsi
really is suspect or if she just dislikes him.

Has the next day's itinerary been, in fact, decided?
And whose decision is it anyway? In these moments,
Annette is unaware that she is balanced on a ridge
because it is engulfed in a fog that will only lift
much later. We see her, a precipice on either side,
looking straight ahead without hesitation. She pictures
her two young sons, Gillou and Jean-Ri, and
the baby girl, still unnamed, sleeping an embryo's
sleep beneath her heart. She sees the Mediterranean's
intense blue and Joe, the father of her children.
Then darkness falls.

The next morning, she is driving to Paris with
Georges, by far her favourite. For once, he has insisted on
a particular route. This is all the more curious because
until now he always let her decide on the itinerary, and
for the last six months or more they've driven
the length and breadth of France on minor and back roads
without concern. Yet on this one day he imposed
the route, which seems – obvious, in retrospect – connected
to the letter from Paul the day before.

It's destiny, they say. But now that destiny has struck and
cannot be changed, we'll take two minutes for a brief aside.
The trunk road Annette and Georges are driving on

is the legendary 'Holiday Route' that runs straight from
    Paris
to the Côte d'Azur, made famous in 1959 when it was brand
    new
by Charles Trenet's hit song named after it: 'Nationale Sept'.
If you take Route Seven south from Paris you'll end, with it,
at the sea. If you kept going straight ahead, with water
instead of asphalt under your wheels, you'd reach
another continent. And if you continued two thousand
kilometres more in the same direction on this new land mass,
you'd come to southern Algeria, in a small Berber village
not mentioned in Trenet's song: Tamanrasset. Here,
in this remote place or near it, in February 1960 – three
    months
after the day Annette and Georges drove north on Route
    Seven –
France tested its first atomic bomb. Called *Gerboise bleu*,
Blue Jerboa, it was three times more powerful than
the perversely named Little Boy, dropped on Hiroshima.
As everyone knows, even those who have never seen
these little rodents, jerboas are not blue. Predictably,
they're the colour of sand to blend in with their
    surroundings.
The only blue things in the desert are the indigo turbans,
or *cheches*, worn by the Tuareg people who have lived in
the Sahara since ancient times, hence the name 'Blue People'
given them by the Europeans. Thousands of Tuareg,
including many women and children, would perish.

How many dead or contaminated? No counts were kept,
no Trenet would sing about the dead. Tamanrasset.
They died too far from the Nationale Sept.

In early November '59, Georges and Annette are arrested
on the legendary motorway. From a passing Mercedes
three pairs of eyes drill into them and that is that. A few
hundred metres further on, a spike strip is spread across
the road. All right, all right; Annette brakes and has just
    enough
time to ask, 'What's your name again?' She doesn't mean
his code name Georges or his real name but the one
on his false identification papers. She doesn't catch it,
something ending in *-bert*: Robert, maybe? Or Albert?
Annette only learns his actual name in prison and
can honestly tell the police she'd never heard it before:
Mohamed Daksi. What the police don't tell her, probably
because they don't know, is what her own name is. They
still haven't figured out who the woman is behind her
false ID. In the meantime, they address her as 'Madame'
but treat Daksi with condescension. He's an Arab,
she is not; no need for an investigation to figure that out.
Her large key ring's final hiding place, or better,
grave, is a pit latrine. To reach the keys' last resting place,
a guard leads her across a courtyard where, to her surprise,
she sees her disassembled car 'spread out like laundry
in a field' (to quote Annette). She thinks of her boys and
what fun they would have had helping the mechanic

with this task. Suddenly, the world turns dark. What had
once been her future is now nothing more than a long,
empty stretch of dead time, devoid of children's laughter,
of passion, of deep breaths of sea air. She sees it all before her,
because she finally can see, and she knows. Did she not
know before? Was she blind? She did know, yet took the risk.
She even knew with reasonable accuracy how many years
of her life Algerian independence and her own
independence as a woman would cost her if she
were charged. But what exactly does it mean to know?
Of course, we know any time we drive a car
that we could have an accident and lose life or limb.
We know perfectly well but don't think about it, or no one
would ever get behind the wheel. Would Annette have
    joined
the Resistance if she had known – in that most profound
    sense
of knowing, not just having a vague idea about something
but experiencing it body and soul – if, then, she had known
what torture is or being gassed or execution by firing squad?

Fortunately, however, the future is only present as
the succeeding moment, and this momentary future
requires presence of mind. For Annette, now, under arrest,
this means getting through the day without revealing
a single name, not her own or anyone else's that
could put them on the track of her husband who,
this very day, is transporting a suitcase through Paris.

The two boys are at home with their back-up parents, Élise
and Lucien; their real father is on the road, their mother
in a cell or an interrogation room
in the episcopal palace of Marseille, which has housed
the headquarters of the police ever since the separation
of Church and State at the beginning of the century.
She's called 'Arabs' whore' with a few slaps for emphasis.
Another officer, this one with better manners, comes
to question her. She explains to him – or tries her best to –
why she opposes the oppression of other countries and
their inhabitants and why she has sided with the FLN.
She talks and talks and suddenly it's as if she were
'face to face with herself' (to quote Annette), and what
she sees, from outside herself, is a rather ridiculous,
grandiloquent but not very persuasive person, of whom
she can be proud. The officer merely shrugs.

Her house is searched. Six or seven policemen upend
absolutely everything but her unshakeable convictions.
Annette knows that what she did is just even if justices
may not agree. She doesn't have a single doubt.
Should she? While the police are emptying drawers and
flipping mattresses and Annette is trying to make the
    children
understand that she will shortly have to leave again with these
removal men, we'll glance at the many books stacked
mutely on her shelves which she and Joe have collected
and read over the years. The officers take a few books

off the shelves and shake them. But there are so many
they soon give up. While their backs are turned,
let's pick up one that certainly could have been there
even if it was not actually there at the time:
Albert Camus' *Algerian Chronicles*. Opening it,
we read, 'No matter what cause one defends, it will forever
be disgraced by the blind massacre of an innocent crowd
when the killer knows in advance that women and children
    will die.'
Let's slip it back onto the shelf and take another: Rousseau.
'Nothing on this earth is worth buying at the price
of human blood.' And a third by the anarchist Kropotkin
with his account of the assassination of the tsar:
'There Alexander II lay upon the snow, profusely bleeding,
abandoned by every one of his followers! All had
disappeared. It was cadets, returning from the parade,
who lifted the suffering Tsar from the snow and put him
in a sledge, covering his shivering body with a cadet mantle
and his bare head with a cadet cap. And it was one of
the terrorists, Emelianoff, with a bomb wrapped in paper
under his arm, who, at the risk of being arrested on the spot
and hanged, rushed with the cadets to help the wounded man.'
End of the quotations, for now. And perhaps the beginning
of something else? Of doubt? No. Beyond the doubts
that penetrate consciousness there are others seething
in a distant pool. Is it love that makes a revolutionary,
or is it hatred? Is it ideas or some living thing
that shakes to the core those faced with someone in misery,

someone who is starving, who is suffering, or… has lost
their legs to a bomb and will not survive? While the police
rifle through her closets, Annette watches her children playing
and knows she won't see them again for a long time.
Perhaps she has no thoughts in her head, just a pervasive
pain and the extraordinary effort it takes not to cry
in front of the children and to pretend everything
is fine. No one can see into the darkness in another's head
and certainly not into one's own, but in these long
moments perhaps inaudible questions are forming:
Is what I did right? Was it worth it? Yes? No?

Could this struggle have achieved its goal without
violence? In the late thirties, Camus, who was born
in Algeria, wrote about the misery in Kabylia,
the exploitation, the slave labour, even. Others
had demanded reforms, equal rights, but to little effect,
not to say no effect at all. It took exploding bombs
for the French government slowly, much too slowly,
and only slightly, to modify its politics. There was Gandhi,
     true,
and later South Africa. Some patient souls believe
that violence begets only violence and they'd rather
sit in prison for years than harm a single hair
on an exploiter's head. Who could blame those who have
lost patience? Camus, for one. He's no descendant
of the colonizing landowners, exploiters and parasites;
indeed, many of the French in Algeria are poor themselves

even if richer than their Arab neighbours. Annette knows
all this, but what has stirred her up is something else,
it's a principle, and principles put one in the right
or in the wrong. This particular principle puts her
in the right in saying that no nation has the right
to subjugate another. Camus says the same but adds,
'People are now planting bombs on tramways in Algiers.
My mother could be on one of them. If that is justice,
I prefer my mother.' Can't one have both, one's mother and
justice? With luck, yes. And what does Frantz Fanon say?
'For the colonized, life can only emerge from the rotting
corpse of the colonizer.' That is from *The Wretched
of the Earth* with a preface by Sartre, but hang on…
could such a preface represent another kind
of tutelage, even colonizing, or not? Even with
the prefaced author's consent. In it, Sartre writes,
'For in the initial phase of a revolt, killing is necessary.
To slaughter a European is to kill two birds with
one stone, to do away in one blow with both oppressor
and oppressed: leaving one dead and the other free.'
Sartre seems to have forgotten that he himself
is a European.

Paradoxically, now that Annette has time
for such reflections, it's too late. The trap – and
the handcuffs – have snapped shut. The newspapers
and news magazines are salivating over the easy
prey. A Frenchwoman, a doctor, no less,

watching over and helping an Arab – the poor woman
must be in some kind of sexual thrall to the stud.
Words are put into her mouth: I'd have done anything
for him! And this cliché is printed next to a large
photograph of her, stolen by one of the officers
searching her home (what's wrong with a bit of profit
on the side?). Dozens of reporters, the paper says,
fanned out through the bars and nightclubs of Marseille
in search of details about her tawdry life. Unfortunately
no one remembers ever having seen Annette except
for the owner of a restaurant where she occasionally
had a meal… always alone with a book in hand.
Very dodgy. *France-Soir* calls her 'the FLN's sutler',
with clear overtones of prostitution. They barely mention
that she fought in the Resistance, and only then
as the source of her mania for aliases. The journalists
spill much more ink on what appears to them a greater
mystery, one that cannot be explained by passion alone:
how does a perfectly respectable doctor and scientist,
but above all a daughter-in-law of a highly respected
neurologist and professor of medicine, a doctor's wife
and mother of future doctors or similarly honourable
professionals, how does such a woman who has everything,
especially her good reputation, to lose get entangled
with such sinister and impecunious figures?

In the interrogations, she needs all her strength and
her shrewdness to clear Joe from any guilt – even though,

despite his reservations and misgivings he has, in fact,
rendered services to the FLN – and to deflect
any suspicion from Élise and Lucien, even though
they have housed some Algerian members of the
    movement.
These three absolutely must remain at liberty. Who else
would take care of her children when she's in prison?
It works. Then come fourteen days of solitary
confinement, during which she feels like Prisypkin
from Mayakovsky's *Bedbug*, who was kept in a freezer
for fifty years. She knows nothing of what's happening
in the outside world or even in the prison itself.
Nor is she aware that everyone in the prison
knows almost all there is to know about her. And so
one day when Annette is in isolation, a fellow prisoner,
handing out meals under the eye of a guard, slips her
an unusually large piece of bread and gives her
a direct look. Four cigarettes, matches, a nail file and
a heart-shaped piece of soap. Isn't that nice? Someone
is thinking of her. And this someone signs three names
on the wrapping: Nadia, Halima, Zineb. Annette
has only just arrived in prison and already has
three unknown friends, Algerians who want to thank her
with these gifts and show her that within these dark
and hostile walls she is neither alone nor forgotten.
It's her first signal from the human world in ten days.
Before long she meets these new friends and three other
political prisoners, recently extradited from Algeria.

Among them is Djamila Bouhired, who is considered
a heroine in Algeria and treated accordingly in France.
She fought in the Battle of Algiers, although to her
frustration, the bombs she planted did not explode.
She was wounded, captured and tortured but
did not reveal her leader's name: Saadi Yacef.
Yacef would later re-enact his own role better in a film
(soundtrack: Johann Sebastian Bach and Ennio
Morricone) than in real life. Meanwhile, in prison
Djamila plays her role with great conviction.
Her lawyer, Jacques Vergès, presents her as the 'soul
of terrorism', then as the face of the Algerian
revolution, and eventually makes her his wife.
Annette doesn't much care for Vergès and hires instead
two lawyers who are friends of hers. The three Algerians
from Algeria, of which Djamila is one,
consider themselves superior to those who,
like Nadia and Halima, didn't fight on Algerian
soil but lived in France and fought for the cause there.
True, they were involved in the attacks on
the Mourepiane and Lavéra oil refineries,
which left nineteen wounded and one dead. But those
don't compare to the attacks in Algeria and,
in fact, only Djamila is sentenced to death.
Then pardoned two years later. Whereas Annette...

But we are getting ahead of ourselves, as the saying
goes, because a month in prison can seem endless,

all the more so when it's followed by a second,
then a third… To the prison administration's
astonishment, Annette is engrossed in the memoirs
of General de Gaulle. She also reads *Le Monde*,
but above all she reads the hearts and souls of the guards and
her fellow prisoners, from the prostitute and
the peasant woman who used an axe to stop
her husband's violent abuse to the post-office worker
who relieved the billion-franc national lottery purse
of a few banknotes. Annette becomes the go-to person
for any and all who have secrets or problems of any sort
with their children, their husbands or their bunions. Zineb,
one of the terrorists, dreams of becoming Miss Algeria,
although she'd settle for Miss Marseille, which proves
that she's not driven solely by nationalism. A curious lot.
Several prisoners never open their mouths. Depression.

Confined with Algerians, Annette realizes
that she is fighting for a country she knows nothing
about. In other words, she's not advocating
for a nation but for grand ideas and the principles of
equality and self-determination. Is this even possible?
Can you really fight, even die, for ideas? Do ideas
that are fought for remain ideas? Don't they tend
to congeal into something real, into people,
administrative systems, bodies of laws,
flesh and blood? It occurs to her that she has fought
for a reality she knows only from newspaper

reports. True, she did go to Algeria once,
to visit friends. But the Algerians she met then
were mostly household staff. Here, in prison, the staff
are French (and very French at that: they simply don't
do as they're told). Annette is on the side
of the Algerians and criminals. From them she learns
a great deal about their country. Djamila
is a particularly gifted storyteller (no, we're not
going to mention A *Thousand and One Nights*).
Some discussions become heated, and Djamila
is always ready to set others straight. She doesn't
tolerate contradiction. She's a heroine with
a heroine's self-confidence. As close to
an embodiment of the revolution as could be,
there's no one better placed than Djamila to explain
what kind of revolution it is, what its origins
and its likely outcomes are. And if she were to embody
the truth as well, no one would bat an eyelid. She is
intelligent and, above all, a good prison comrade.

Then Christmas comes. Annette is on good terms
with the director, who allows the political prisoners
to eat Christmas dinner together. From her oven at home
Annette conjures up a turkey with chestnut dressing
(roasted by Élise). She also manages to produce
a *bûche de noël*, the rich, log-shaped holiday cake.
As the authority on religious questions, Djamila
has sanctioned this traditional dinner, provided

the turkey has been slaughtered according to
the rules. So the turkey comes from a halal butcher,
surely an unusual source for a Christmas roast.
The women are bubbling with joy – until Djamila asks
about the gravy and about the oven's religion.
Okay, okay, that's not exactly how she puts it, but
she does question if the oven and gravy are permissible
under Islamic dietary laws. They aren't. The turkey
is forbidden. Djamila seems to have set her mind on
spoiling this small and essentially profane feast.
(Besides, they weren't eating halal food in prison
on any other days. Why insist on that one day?)

All are asleep except Annette, who lies awake
in tears. Perhaps she is thinking of her husband's
warning two years earlier, when he voiced concern
about the growing influence of Islam within
the Algerian independence movement. Annette
had not witnessed any of this in Georges, the leader
who was arrested with her, and among the Algerian
communists, religion did not seem of primary
importance. Aren't we humans all rather similar,
and when we're not – don't we strive to become so?
Religions do not unite, they divide. Then again,
what was she thinking when she decided to serve
her Muslim friends such an overtly Christian
meal? The answer is that for her it had nothing to do
with religion, it was simply an occasion to feel less alone

and share some joy. Annette saw it one way and
Djamila saw it another because before landing in prison,
she had lived in a country that was ninety per cent Muslim
and one hundred per cent of the holidays were Christian.
Maybe refusing Annette's turkey was Djamila's way
of saying keep your palm fronds, Easter eggs and Christmas
geese! That could be. Back in her cell, Annette sees only
intransigence, rejection and hostility towards herself
even though she's clearly on Djamila's side. But what if
it's not clear to Djamila? Can Annette ever truly be
on Djamila's side, no matter how many years she spends
in prison, or even if she dies for Algerian independence,
if she was born on the wrong side, the side of the oppressors,
the colonizers? Is it a kind of original sin of which
one can never be washed clean? Annette does not see things
this way. She is Breton but not Catholic. Djamila
is still young and has suffered horrible experiences,
so now is stubborn or a little crazy. But in the end,
it's not worth being angry with her over a turkey,
which was shared among the non-political prisoners.

Prison life wouldn't be so bad if, like Annette,
you had your own cell, reading material, visits
and many other activities. It would certainly be
bearable if it weren't for the bars. Anyway.
In the new year, she returns to her research
in neurophysiology (specifically into
myoclonic encephalopathy of infancy

with hypsarrhythmia, should that mean
anything to you). As the piles of books rise,
her belly swells. She is doing well. Still,
now and again she suffers bouts of pure misery.
She thinks of Gillou and Jean-Ri – no, *thinks*
is not the right word, she can barely marshal
her thoughts – the boys are so real to her,
she believes she is hugging and kissing them
even though every cell in her body is telling her
that her children are not with her and won't be
any time soon. Actually, she's the one
who won't be where, according to her feelings and
social conventions, she belongs. Instead,
she'll be imprisoned in this or some other jail.

In this situation, could she have any desire,
any urge other than to get out? The only thing
that could unlock a door for her is her growing
belly. With its help, Annette's lawyers Kiejman and
Vidal-Naquet try to secure a pretrial release and delay
the trial if possible. As long as de Gaulle refuses
to negotiate with the FLN, the fighters and those
who assist them are considered terrorists. Nonetheless,
despite all the assurances to the contrary, by spring
it has become clear that negotiations will take place.
And, in fact, the first are held in June.
Public opinion, that gossipy, fickle creature,
shifts sides, a bit more each day, such that

the later the trial date, the less Annette will be seen
as a terrorist and the more she'll be admired
as fighting for a just cause. But how could her trial be
postponed? As swollen as her belly is, it's still
not enough. They'll need yet another ruse.
Her pregnancy must be deemed high-risk, even though
that's not actually the case. Ailments promptly
set in. Annette is transferred to a hospital (aptly
named l'Hôpital de la Conception) and kept
under guard, of course. Examinations, specialists,
doctors. The court appoints the latter, but
the hospitals also have doctors on staff with different
views. One is nice enough to exchange Annette's
specimen with that of a patient in terrible health.
High-risk pregnancy! Life-threatening complications!
On 2 June, there is good news: Annette is granted
house arrest until the birth and the upcoming trial.
Officers are posted at her house day
and night. So what? She's free!

At home, there's a celebration, lots of people,
noise, bouquets, clinking glasses and excitement.
It sends half of Annette's mind spinning, the half
that is not still in prison. For a moment, she misses
the quiet of her cell. Everything will be all right!
Rather, it won't end too badly. She feels the baby
thrashing, as eager to get out as she was to escape
her cell. A few days later, the birth goes smoothly,

despite the feared complications. Myriam,
a little girl with adorable, crinkly eyes. Summer
comes. Annette has no inkling that it will be her last.
Not the last summer of her long life, no, but the last
of its kind, a summer filled with family, lively
children, their sorrows and joys. It all ends
with the last hot days of summer, even though
she has just borne her third child and it could all
turn out differently. Couldn't it?

In autumn, the two accused, Annette and Mohamed
Daksi, alias Georges, are called before the court.
Officially, the country is not at war, but
there is a state of emergency and therefore
the court is a military tribunal. The two lawyers
don't lose any time. They search for avenues,
arguments, strategies, but can they explain
to the officers, the ones who are fighting this war
(or 'events') that it is unjust and wrong? Most
of the suitcase carriers in the *réseau Jeanson*,
to which Annette did and still does belong,
were sentenced a few weeks earlier (except
for Jeanson himself, who disappeared with his own
suitcase in time). Most of her friends in the network
were given ten years and, on reflection, there's no reason
for Annette to be given a shorter sentence. In truth,
they could skip the testimonies and the impressive
closing arguments, but they don't give up any

opportunity to show the officers that this is
a new case of resistance against an occupying
power and resistance should be rewarded with
medals, not incarceration. It's clear to the lawyers
that their trouble will be for naught.

The trial will be held in the Fort Saint-Nicolas,
a fortress that looms high above the port, built by
Louis XIV to subdue recalcitrant Marseille.
Will the military tribunal succeed within these walls
in subduing Daksi and his accomplice Annette?
When the first day of the trial arrives, nothing exists
in this world for Annette but a tooth. The sudden
inflammation of a wisdom tooth has enveloped her
in a cloud of pain more formidable than any fortress,
army or king. As she sits trapped in the cave
of her mouth, the character witnesses appear one
after the other and paint a magnificent portrait
(without swollen cheeks). Taking the witness box
are Alfred Fessard, eminent neurologist and
professor at the Collège de France; Gestaut, Annette's
superior in the hospital; many of her colleagues…
and Simone and Daniel, the two children whose lives
she saved, no longer children but in their thirties.
Not much of what they say penetrates her cloud
of pain, but it does reach those of us who are in
the audience or would have liked to be. Simone
testifies that her rescuer is a born saviour,

like her parents before her. The entire family
helps and saves and lends a hand to outcasts
and the humiliated. She recalls how one day
Annette picked up someone sprawled on the ground
and rushed him to hospital in a taxi, while onlookers
preferred to insist, in order to soothe their consciences
and avoid inconvenience, that he was simply
sleeping off his drink. The high-ranking officers
are not moved. They are judging acts of terrorism
and subversion. The members of the FLN are not
harmless drunks. Daksi, the electrician from Constantine,
sits behind her on a bench, as upright and dignified
as a king of Numidia. He was already seated there
when Annette was escorted by two guards to her seat
in the row right in front of his. When she turned
to greet him, he stood and kissed her hand, the perfect
gesture for any movie adaptation of his life.

After two or three days, a judgment is reached.
Her case is clear, as it was from the beginning when
she admitted – or rather, proudly asserted – that she had
served the FLN with full knowledge and of her own
free will. Her small team of lawyers one and two,
several friends and Joe had come up with a solution
long before. It has been planned and arranged. All
that remains is to carry it out. But is escape really
the best solution? What about Joe? The children?
What will become of them? Will they follow her?

She could almost get used to prison, she tells
herself (but no one else: what if they took her
at her word?). True enough, in any case,
for the Baumettes prison, where she had been once before
and where she has found friends and a rhythm
of life. But to stay for ten years? She'll certainly
get that many. That's more than she could bear. Only one
option remains, but she will have to move fast and
act while she is still under guard and not yet
locked up behind thick stone walls. She must escape
before the verdict is reached and her house arrest
suspended. During the trial, she has faithfully
worn the bronze-coloured suit, in the lapels of which
Nadia has carefully sewn good luck charms
made of substances like dried placenta powder.
Although she has no time for superstition, Annette
takes joy in fingering the friendly lining during
the long hours of the trial. But it's no help:
she must escape. The plan is set, but there's time
for a short digression before she sets out:

The apartment where Annette is under house arrest
is in the building owned by her *grand bourgeois*
parents-in-law. Joe's father, as has been mentioned,
was an eminent doctor. His very dominating and
eccentric mother was a descendant of a Russian Jewish
diamond merchant from Odessa and she had a few spare
gems. Their lifestyle was far from modest; for a time

they employed a chauffeur, a Russian like his boss,
who suddenly quit when he got married.
Some months later, perhaps a year, the elder
Madame Roger opened her safe to put away
some jewellery she almost always wore and what
did she find? Nothing. A void, the empty object
of a conception of jewels that Kant calls
nihil privativum, or, simply put: theft.
The police were called. When they inspected
every inch of the building with professional eyes,
they did, in fact, find something in a dark
corner of the basement: no jewels, alas, but
a mattress and a camping stove. They also discovered
a door no one had previously noticed, much less
used. The police had only to stand guard behind it
and arrest the first to enter. It was the former chauffeur,
no surprise, without the jewels, of course. He'd sold them
long before. In the years since then, no one has needed
the small, inconspicuous door. Until now. Until
Annette needs an escape and immediately
remembers the door that opens onto an alley
behind the house, neglected by the police.

Is Annette having second thoughts? Does she still hesitate?
Not at all; her mind is made up. The children
will follow later. It's all arranged. There are no other
alternatives to ponder, all the options have been weighed.
At an earlier point there might have been time

for consideration, it might have been possible
to divert the course of events but now, three days
before her sentencing, it's too late for anything but
flight. The newborn girl will stay behind, as will
the two boys, along with Joe, in whose arms
they were all conceived.

One September morning in 1960, a figure
with newly darkened hair and dark eyebrows,
not traits one finds in Brittany, slips out of
the cellar door and climbs into a car passing by
as if by chance – not in the front seat nor in
the back, but in the boot, which is no bigger
than a vegetable crate. Still, folded up like
a jackknife, Annette fits into the tiny space.
In this crate, she'll reach the airport, where,
aside from planes, there are large car parks
filled with cars. There, she can discreetly change
vehicles. Annette gets into the passenger seat
of a car with Swiss plates, driven by Suzanne,
a friend who lives in Paris but is from Geneva.
Suzanne drives Annette to a village very near
the last hurdle, i.e. the Swiss border. In this
village, somewhere between Annemasse and
Thonon-les-Bains, they meet Suzanne's mother and
sister, who live on the other side of the border
and have just driven through the checkpoint. They
regularly cross the border and the guards are used

to seeing their faces behind the windscreen.
From this point everything will be easy – as easy
as many such situations often look in retrospect.
Suzanne's sister hands Annette her coat along with
sunglasses and a scarf, which Annette wraps
like a turban around her head as a fashion statement
but also because that's how her friend's sister wears it.
Annette gets into the car with Suzanne's mother,
and soon after – night is already falling – she gives
the guards a friendly wave as she crosses the border.

Bern Milan Rome then straight to Tunis, where
the not yet governing Algerian government
is based. Annette's efforts to bring freedom and
justice to everyone drive her ever further south – Dinan,
Lyon, Marseille and now a leap to Tunis – as if,
in addition to a cardinal point, South were a kind of
political Arcadia, free of tyranny and exploitation,
another name for that never-seen ancient land
of which so many have long dreamed. The coast
of Brittany, where Annette was born, like that
of northern Africa, faces north.

Tunis, then. Everything here is unknown to Annette
and all are strangers. Yet the reverse is not true.
Within hours, or at most a few days, the entire medina
knows that this woman supported the FLN. She
is offered more Turkish delight than she could

eat in a lifetime. In Marseille, she is sentenced
in absentia to ten years in prison, and soon afterwards
the headline ANNETTE ROGER IN TUNIS blares next
to a photograph of her taken without her knowledge
in front of the headquarters of the FLN.
She would have preferred to remain incognito.
Isn't it rather gratifying, after months in prison,
followed by escape and exile, to receive gratitude
for what she has done? Not at all. It is now
fifteen years since Annette was Nobody, but
she was never able to completely banish that
self-effacement. Sooner or later it would drive her
back underground, into all sorts of hiding places,
into a clandestine existence. Furthermore,
as difficult as life is without an identity, it becomes
like a nest, like a night in which one feels at home,
and is not easy to abandon from one day
to the next. In her Tunisian exile, she is an owl
hurled into daylight, but as soon as she is settled
and can take action again, attacking evil head-on, her
   nightmare
fades. And the newspapers have already moved on.
But what will happen to her next?

Until very recently she was pregnant, held her
tiny daughter in her arms, and, until now, she had her sons
and husband with her, along with mostly meaningful work,
but now: nothing. She could easily fall into this abyss,

but no, not Annette. She keeps running relentlessly,
as if she still had firm ground under her feet,
her legs spinning like those of cartoon characters
running off cliffs. She's a doctor, and doctors
always have much to do, especially in a country
like Tunisia that has only been independent
for four years and on whose borders
the FLN's armies are camped. Annette is busy
everywhere at once: in the hospital in Tunis,
where she takes over the position of Frantz Fanon
and his colleagues, on the border, in the small city
of El-Kef and in the National Liberation Army's camps,
where as many wounds as disillusionments await her.
She recalls that what drove her to support the FLN
were reports of the French army torturing prisoners
exactly as the Gestapo had tortured Resistance fighters
to make them talk. Now she sees that the FLN
does the same. They're not fighting solely for
independence, but also for power. They torture
their rivals and those who disagree, but also
simple soldiers who would otherwise refuse
to fight, that is, they are ready to fight and even
to die fighting, but not to enter a pointless
deadly obstacle course. For in order to cut off
the internal FLN (internal because based in Algeria,
which is part of France) from its bases in Tunisia,
the French army has built a death strip along
the border filled with mines, barbed wire and

electric fences. The FLN decided to drive
dissenters through this gruesome stretch of land.
The few who were not shredded by mines or
electrified were shot as soon as they reached
the other side. Those who find it wiser to stay put
are tortured. Perhaps. It's not systematic
and may even be the exception. But for Annette,
just once is too much. Did she do all she has done
and sacrifice everything dear to her
(only provisionally, she still believes at this point)
just to exchange one torture for another in the end?

Annette longs to give it all up. And she quits –
but then is persuaded to change her mind. Would the sick
and the wounded be better off without her? And
as cruel and repugnant as these methods are,
independence remains an undisputedly just
and good cause and all the mistakes and crimes
that have been committed, as they always are,
cannot change that. But why? Why such abuses?
Are they inevitable? Always the eggs broken
for the omelette? She doesn't know, still hesitates.

In the end, she stays. Does she have a choice?
If she left, she'd have to admit that she was wrong,
that she might have been too impulsive, that her zeal
for action, her anger may have deluded her
about a reality that she did not and could not know

and deluded her about a country she would only
learn about from a distance and at a remove?
Perhaps. But neither she nor anyone else can
decide if that is true or not because to do so
does not require an internal or external judge
but the possibility of taking back a move
as in a friendly game of chess.

The many directions life can take
have one thing in common: they all point forward.
And ahead there is action, assuaging, organizing,
healing. There is so much, so terribly much to do
in this land that is not yet a nation and never was one.
Nationhood was only ever a hope, a desire. She
doesn't only have to deal with poor devils but also
with those who will be in power later: Ferhat Abbas,
provisional ruler of this non-existent country,
Boumédiène, who leads an army that very much
exists, Boussouf, well-informed about all goings-on,
and Bouteflika, who will rule the country
forty to sixty years later, already half-dead and
probably its president even when completely dead.
From this group of uncracked eggs, a nomenklatura
will emerge several years later. Annette still dreams
of a socialist country, new and just, and does not
suspect – nor does she want to suspect – what these men
will later make of it. She dreams of an ideal place,
a place she has been working towards for more than half

149

her life, but one that does not exist, just as this new
Algeria does not exist. Unlike Algeria, it never will.

There is her dream of a good country, but she also
has a dream of a good life with her children finally
at her side again. It had been agreed before she fled
that Joe would bring them to her as soon as possible.
He has a position in Marseille that he doesn't want to leave,
so he has planned to see visit Annette and the children
as often as he can. It's only a matter of crossing the
Mediterranean. They can manage for a while,
why not – the war can't go on forever and then
there will be an amnesty. They'll be reunited.
That was the hope and the plan, so as soon as she arrived,
Annette began searching for a place for the family to live,
where the children would have their own rooms.
She even finds a nanny, since she has so much work to do.
Their father needs only bring the children as far as Rome,
that's the plan, that's what they'll do – and he tries. But he
is stopped with the boys at the Italian border. Prohibited
from leaving the country. How can that be? He hasn't broken
any laws. (In fact, he has: he also carried suitcases
for the FLN, but the State could never prove it so charges
were dropped.) Regardless, they don't let him through.
In France, the 'events' hold sway and the police and the
     courts
take some latitude with the law. If they don't want
to let someone leave the country, that's the way it is,

whether or not he has young children and a wife
stuck abroad. What do they care?

There are dreams. And there is waking. In this new life,
of which she had never dreamed, you can't – she can't –
have it all: fighting for a better world, braving all kinds
of dangers, having children. Well, as for having children,
of course she can, but raising them, watching them play
and grow, hugging and kissing them, that she cannot do.
Three months after her escape, Annette finally wakes fully
to the fact that she may have lost her three children forever.
Ten years! In ten years, the boys will almost be grown;
the newborn girl, Myriam, will never have seen her mother,
or only in a timeless reverie. When she finally sees Annette,
Myriam will look at her as at a complete stranger,
or as a new neighbour at best. For the first time
in decades, Annette would rather die. To hell
with the FLN and all the Algerians, to hell with
de Gaulle and the communists. To hell with the lot.
And to hell a thousand times herself.

Dreams are tenacious. They don't die after a few weeks
of darkness and drought. Annette is soon weaving new plans
to meet her family a few months later, as soon as summer
returns: not on land but on the Mediterranean Sea, perhaps?
The borders are closely guarded, but isn't it mostly water
that separates her from her children? What about a boat?
Couldn't they reunite at sea? She would come

from Tunisia, Joe and the children from Marseille.
And if that is not possible, there is still the hope
that this war will end with an independent Algeria
and, eventually, an amnesty.

Times will come, will inevitably arrive, with room enough
for reflection, a vast expanse of time she can devote
to thought, and it will be a torment. But at the moment
there is much too much to do and thinking is a brake.
In any case, the die is cast. Annette can no longer
change course. She pins her hopes on next summer,
on seeing her children. In the meantime, she works.
She thinks that her work does not put her in danger,
and realizes only later that she was and is at risk.
In the winter of '59–'60, at the home
of the Chaulets, who are French and fighting for
the FLN like her, Annette hears a voice
coming from so high above her that, were she
a believer, she might have thought God was speaking
to her. But she believes only in human reason,
although she has very little reason left once
her eyes have travelled up the speaker's long torso
and finally met that person's eyes. In short,
that is it for Annette. There are such flashes
of the heart that don't wait for the right moment
but simply strike as they will. Annette is struck
that day in the Chaulets' corridor. So is the man,
named Amara, who is as tall as Annette is short.

He is Algerian and, like all Algerians in Tunisia,
he is with the FLN.

From this moment on, everything will be different;
this is a swerve within an immanent turn and it will
colour Annette's memory of Tunis and Tunisia,
which will be forever illuminated by the light
she perceived in the plane before even setting foot
in the country, the dusty sunlight in which flocks
of flamingoes flutter.

Annette eventually learns from Amara himself
that although she imagines she is now in friendly
territory and safe from pursuit or persecution,
she would be a thousand times safer in prison. Amara
is not just her lover and friend, but her protector
as well. Isn't that the case with all who love,
no matter who they are? No doubt, but not exactly
in the same sense. Amara is in charge of her safety
and has secretly been protecting her directly and
indirectly for some time now without her knowing.
Is her life in danger? There is, of course, that group
that calls itself the Red Hand. Contrary to what
one might think, they are not Reds but spillers of blood.
The Red Hand are happy to slay fighters for the FLN,
the lawyers who defend them, those who deliver them arms
and all who help in any way. But surely not a little fish
like Annette? Annette thinks she is a much smaller

fish than others, especially France, deem her to be.
She was given a sentence of ten years, after all.
Speaking of France: many years later, it came out
that the Red Hand was not some group of demented,
ultra-right colonialists as had always been claimed, but an arm
of the French government. The hand that could
make anyone it wished disappear with impunity
was in fact the French secret service. This group of
demented, ultra-right colonialists did exist. Its code name
was Red Hand, but its real name was France.

With Amara's help and a lot of luck, Annette escapes
her own country's murderous hand. There is only one
victim in her inner circle, and it's a box of chocolates.
The chocolates are fine Belgian pralines sent to her
in her Tunisian exile all the way from Liège. Because
a strange noise or ticking seems to be coming from the box,
it is carefully deactivated with a shot from a distance.
For those who know that others have died from similar gifts,
the situation is less comical. One such package, destined
for Annette, was intercepted by her protectors before it reached
her. It, too, was deactivated at the far end of the garden.

Annette works. She is regularly on duty
at the FLN offices. One day, a visitor named Younsi
is announced. 'Younsi who? I don't know any Younsis.'
A patient, maybe? The door opens and 'fireballs ricochet
in her chest' (Annette's words). The man entering the room

is none other than Paul, the man she knew as Paul in France,
the one who betrayed her and Daksi eighteen months
before. Because of him they were caught
on the Nationale Sept. She has no concrete proof,
but more than mere suspicion. This is not a question
of intuition, feminine or otherwise. How could
the police be aware of things known only to Daksi
and Annette? Only Daksi and she – and this
Younsi – knew she was pregnant, for example.
And why did he behave so suspiciously when
he wasn't suspected of anything? He informed on them,
without a doubt. There are more than enough dots
to connect. The fact that she is thousands of kilometres
from her children, that she sat in prison for half a year and
nine and a half more years wait for her in France,
that everything, absolutely everything in her life
has changed and not because she wanted change, is due
to this man without character and with a deceitful bent
who let himself be bought by the French secret service.
The fact that Mohamed Daksi, whom Annette knew as
Georges and whose liaison officer she was for a time,
is still in prison in France, having been sentenced
to ten years like her but unlike her is unable
to escape – all this and much more, Annette is convinced,
goes on this Younsi's account. And now he stands,
in the doorway with that mawkish grin of his.
What should she do? For the moment, nothing.
She sends him on his way.

But she does have a word with two 'Boussouf Boys'.
This is no pop group but the espionage and counter-espionage service of an Algeria that does not officially
exist but which has already formed its police and military
structures. For his own security, rather than that of
the nation, the director of this service, Boussouf himself,
sleeps in a different place every night. As for the
Boussouf Boys, they never sleep. They must always
keep their eyes and ears open. Annette knows two
of them and she tosses the pebble of her suspicions
(or her certitude) into their open ears as into a deep
well – you never know, maybe it will work. She
listens but doesn't hear a sound, not even a
muffled splash. Silence.

She thinks of other things. What else can she do?

A few weeks later, the traitor Paul – or Younsi – is held
by FLN agents north of Paris, in Aubervilliers,
and interrogated for a month and a half. His actual
or suspected denunciation of Daksi and his right hand
is just one accusation among many. One incriminating
circumstance is that after Daksi was betrayed and
imprisoned, Younsi was promoted to his position
as head of *wilaya sud*. As head, it was no trouble
for Younsi to fill other positions with moles and
bring about further arrests. Denunciations.

Embezzlement. Furthermore, he was also accused
of trying to seduce the wives of imprisoned
FLN fighters, then threatening and, despicably,
blackmailing them. During these weeks of captivity
in the Paris suburb and repeated interrogations,
Younsi made confessions that an innocent person
would no doubt have made in similar circumstances.
True enough. But that does not make Younsi innocent.
Far from it. There is no tribunal or lawyer
at his trial. He serves his detention in an apartment
somewhere. He soon realizes what's in store for him
and slits his wrists with a blade after several days.
But dying's not so easy. He'd like them to drive him
into the forest and leave him there to die, but
summary justice has no intention of moving so speedily.
His captors would rather save him, then strangle him
some weeks later. His corpse lands in the Seine
in late June of '62. By then, the war is over;
but the settling of accounts, the purges and so on
have begun in earnest.

Annette opposes the death sentence.

Even in this case?

In every case.

Her indignation, however, is rather moderate.

In the human multitude Annette has already met
or will meet in the coming decades – a veritable ocean
of strangers, acquaintances and intimates – Younsi
is a barely recognizable figure, a fleeting face
she saw a few times in 1959 and once again many
months later, a head that briefly emerged from
the sea of time before being swallowed again
soon after. And yet this insignificant, shadowy
man is the obstacle that derailed her life and
completely changed its course.

After the secret service deactivates the mail bombs,
dangers threaten Annette from the other side: she has
stopped dying her hair dark brown and is once again
a natural blonde. However, in Tunis and Tunisia
in the summer of '61, blonde hair is an affront rather than
an ideal of beauty. It is even a kind of red cloth waved
by the occupiers in front of the occupied. 'The occupied'?
Hasn't Tunis been the capital of a free and sovereign
land for several years? Indeed it has. But whenever France
has withdrawn from a country, the withdrawal is never
complete. It leaves behind many people, a language,
buildings and so on – it digs its claws in wherever
it can, in a small or a sizable part of the country.
In Algeria, later, it will be in the desert. In Tunisia,
France has tried to keep its claws in a spot
that is very small but strategically important:

Fine, fine, we'll leave, on condition that we can keep
Bizerte as a naval base. The Tunisians agree
and for a while, things go well – until they don't.
In the summer of '61, a battle breaks out in which
hundreds are killed, including two dozen Frenchmen.
Shortly after winning, well, the winners finally clear
the field, which is inevitable given that Bizerte
is not in France but in Tunisia. So why the mini-war?
So that France won't lose face, hundreds – primarily
Tunisians – lose their lives. The remaining Tunisians
have had more than enough and don't react well
to the sight of anything that is or looks French. Since
Annette does not advertise in large letters on a T-shirt,
I GOT TEN YEARS FOR HELPING THE FLN!, she is
indistinguishable from the other kind of French
people. She knows who she is and what she thinks
and so doesn't realize the danger she's in until
one evening, when she has left the clinic
and is on her way home. Her car is surrounded
by an angry mob who resent the French. Annette's
Fiat 1100 is easily flipped and, since the police
officer at the scene simply stands by, twiddling
his thumbs, she's flipped inside it. Luckily
she's unhurt, but the shock hits home and from then on
she keeps her hair dyed black. It doesn't always work,
but it gets her through the summer, and in October
the French have won and given in. Bizerte is
Tunisian and Annette is blonde again.

But before then, it's August and Annette is finally
realizing her dream of travelling to Italy to meet
Joe and her children, who will be joining her by boat
(by yacht, to be precise). There are no border controls
at sea and they all arrive, all that is, except the baby,
Myriam, whom the father thought best to leave behind.
Annette's fury turns to sorrow. The little girl is now
one year old, and before her escape Annette had only seen
her daughter for her a few weeks. The children have long
been separated. Myriam doesn't live with her father,
but with Élise and Lucien. Annette's mother, Petite Marthe,
brought Gilles to Brittany. Only the eldest, Jean-Henri,
lives with Joe, although mostly with the neighbours.
The family is torn apart. Annette is too. And now:
they're to gather for a holiday? Indeed, does she have
any other choice? Why spoil what little time she has
with them? Should the three weeks in Portofino also
be sacrificed when so much already has been? She is overjoyed
to see her boys. Joe is a good guy, with an unfortunate tendency
to stray, but Annette can still count on him. Besides,
these past few months she has strayed too. They both know
of each other's affairs. But what should they do with the
    children?
Annette wants all three or none. That may be too much
to ask, and in any case Jean-Ri is not thrilled about going
to Africa without his friends. Then their holiday is over.

But hope springs eternal, and the two friends and spouses
come to a new agreement: when Algeria has gained
independence – it can't be much longer now – and when
she is certain she will stay in this new country,
then the three children will join her.

It can't be much longer and yet it's so far away. At last,
however, Joe suddenly lets her know that in autumn,
Gilles, now nine years old, will be driven across
the Swiss border bundled in the boot of a car
then put on a plane to join her. A friend will help him.
Yes, her son will come! Her joy and hopes are great.
Annette wants to do everything right, to make the boy
feel at home. But perhaps there is no 'right'
when there are so many difficulties. School,
for one. The French schools won't take him
because of his terrorist mother (his false papers
are obviously not good enough). Annette finds
a school for orphans with a wonderful teacher,
but Gilles becomes quarrelsome and taciturn.
The orphans are treated as special cases. They're
called martyrs' children because they lost
their parents in the war. Even though Annette
explains the orphans' situation to her little son
and that he is neither an orphan nor the child
of martyrs, things get worse. On top of that,
the boy becomes gravely ill. Tuberculosis.
No one could reproach Annette more than she does

herself. What kind of mother is she! She drives
those around her mad, her friends, the doctors and
her mother Petite Marthe, who finally takes the boy
to a sanatorium in Yugoslavia. He is healed,
at least his lungs are. He then returns to France
and Annette abandons her hope of being with
her children until she returns from her exile
on the other side of the Mediterranean Sea.

It's already possible to foresee the day when
the Algerian flag is no longer forbidden but
is actually raised throughout the neighbouring
country: after eight years of war, France is about
to declare victory and lose the country, as it already
has lost Tunisia and Morocco, Pondicherry
and Indochina, Senegal, Togo and Chad,
along with other territories because in the long run
people don't like to be deprived of their land
and their rights, even if the divesting is done
by the country of human rights. But for now,
de Gaulle is declaring that France will not
negotiate with terrorists (while conducting
secret talks with the FLN). He also declares
with regard to Ben Bella, who will soon become
the first president of this new nation, that France
will not negotiate with a mere corporal. We
should keep in mind – even at the risk of slightly
delaying the ceasefire – that during the Second

World War, Ben Bella risked his life to free
first Italy, then France and then Germany from
the Germans, that is from those Germans who…
He fought in the deadly battle of Monte Cassino,
in which two of his brothers fell. De Gaulle himself
pinned to Ben Bella's chest the highest distinction
a soldier of his rank can receive. His failure
to be promoted to an officer's rank is due less
to any lack of personal merit than to the fact that
Algerian soldiers in the French army had the right,
even the obligation, to fight and risk their lives
for France, but they were categorically barred
from the officers' ranks. Only one Algerian soldier,
a man by the name of Rafa Ahmed, rose to
brigade general, the very same rank de Gaulle
held (and only temporarily at that). De Gaulle never
served as an army general, a rank he surely
would have reached had he not left for England,
and so on and so forth.

In early 1962, France finally opens official talks
with these gangsters with funny names and low ranks.
In Évian, on Lake Geneva, they agree to a ceasefire,
but the deaths don't cease because the most implacable
colonialist agitators (their covert paramilitary
arm is the OAS, the Secret Armed Organization)
see the ceasefire as a cover for self-determination
and lash out in a blind fury. The mayor of Évian,

for example, is assassinated on the grounds that
he welcomed the negotiators. Because no one knows
who he is and his death was swallowed up in the tide
of hundreds of thousands of casualties in this war,
let us pause for a moment in memory of Camille
Blanc, a socialist, former Resistance fighter and
mayor of the tranquil spa town Évian. Let us pause
on Annette's and therefore our path to a goal
that was also Blanc's but one he would never see:
peace and independence for a new country
whose fate is no longer to be in France's hands
but in the hands of its inhabitants.

The mayor of Évian is dead, but the negotiations
continue and lead to a contract with a clause
stipulating amnesty for all those condemned
in the course of this war. Those who planted bombs,
the leaders of the FLN, even those sentenced
to death in so far as they hadn't been executed,
Saadi Yacef and all the others are released
following the terms of this agreement. But these terms
do not apply to Annette, who, granted, had already
freed herself, but she will have to remain in exile,
separated from her children, for a few more years.
Nor do the terms apply to the other French men and women
who helped the FLN. Only those who served in the army
and engaged in torture are amnestied. Suitcase carriers
and deserters are not pardoned. The FLN

got what they could; the handful of men and women
who fought for them deserve their respect, to be sure,
but they are hardly a priority. Their bad luck.
Perhaps there will soon be another amnesty?
Perhaps. It helps to hope.

Among the liberated prisoners are Annette's friends
from the Baumettes prison, including the embodiment
of Algeria, Djamila Bouhired, the one who disdained
Annette's Christmas turkey but was otherwise
a good comrade in jail. In April 1962, the women
arrive in Tunis, where the founding of the neighbouring
    state
has begun with great conflict. The freed fighters are given
a triumphant welcome and housed in the Villa
Salammbô in the elegant suburb of La Marsa, where
they spread gooey caramel on their legs and
voluptuously tear it off and the little hairs with it. They
bask in their fame and together build a country
in their minds, a socialist Algeria in which they,
the fighters, will have opportunities to be more
than just wives and mothers. They will be deeply
disappointed. Their temporary residence, the Villa
Salammbô, will later house an Institut français,
whose mission is to promote French language and
culture. The villa's name alone is already doing
its part: Flaubert's historical novel *Salammbô*
is named after its main character, who is modelled

on Hamilcar's daughter Salambaal. Once again
we see that when the French leave, they stay.
They truly are everywhere, even where
they don't belong or want to be. The new
Algerian flag, for example, was designed by
a Frenchwoman, a certain Émilie Busquant.

Also among those freed in '62 is the corporal
Ben Bella, imprisoned with four other FLN leaders
since October '56 after the aeroplane they were
travelling on was intercepted by the French secret
services between Morocco and Tunisia. In Tunis,
everyone involved with the FLN knows each other,
and Annette soon meets and speaks with him.
The power structures are still fluid and there are certainly
things Annette doesn't catch even though all those she meets,
all those who have a say speak perfect French, having been
educated in French schools. Will the future leaders
of this nascent state show concern for the masses?
Will they be prepared to share the country's wealth
with all its citizens? Or will the French elite
simply be replaced by an Algerian one? Will the
long-desired independence change anything
for those who hunger for food and education?
Such are the questions Annette asks herself
and those she trusts. Of these, Ben Bella is the only one
who shows any concern for the fellahs or farmers,
the vast majority of this future state, or for women,

who may not be a majority but still constitute half
the population. Annette also feels able to speak
to him about all that worries her, the power struggles,
the clan system and the long-standing custom of
backscratching. She trusts this man. He asks if she has
ideas for the healthcare system. She tells herself
that she might still be some use to this nascent state.
Before long she, too, like his inner circle,
calls Ben Bella 'BB', (*bébé*, as in baby).
Annette is always able to see, or thinks she sees,
beyond the public face and convictions a person displays
and discern if these accord with his or her private self
or are simply donned like a starched shirt. Ben Bella
seems to her an honest man. If he's touched
by the poor farmers' fate, it may be because he is one
himself or his parents were. In any case, Annette gets along
best with those from modest circumstances, as if
poverty improves the character in ways the rich
would like it to. Ben Bella did not learn what he knows
at any university. He was a soldier, a corporal,
an arms dealer, a gunrunner and a gangster
(he robbed a bank in Oran, not to fill his own pockets
but the coffers of the organization that was
the predecessor of the FLN). He spent some years
in prison. He learned quite a bit along the way,
and if he ever had been a simple, modest man,
it's unlikely he remained one. A modest man may well
become a soldier, but is not likely to become a bank robber

or a leader of an underground organization that
is considered a terrorist group. For a time he lived
in Marseille and even scored a goal in the French Cup
when he played with Olympique de Marseille. He is a man
who listens to what he's told – not a common trait.
He's forty-six but still boyish, with a slight
double chin. Annette tells herself: he's a good man.
Perhaps she's right? Furthermore, Ben Bella will
marry late and adopt three children, one of whom
is disabled. Let's be honest: is this the kind of thing
a complete low life would do?

In retrospect – Annette, too, steps outside herself
to look back from a great distance – we think we can discern
something that had previously been hidden by some screen,
by the fog of the present. Thanks to our knowledge
of a time long past that still lies ahead of those alive then,
we believe ourselves qualified to comment,
to shake our heads, to disapprove. For those *in medias res*,
every path is shrouded in fog. And yet it's possible
that Annette in Tunis was more than halfway right:
this man, this Ben Bella, may not be good but
he is not bad; in any case, he's better than many others.
The battles for power are in full swing and
independence is just weeks away. Decades later,
it's still unclear what exactly happened between
the troops stationed along the Tunisian border and
the partisans in the interior of the country, scattered

in various bands of Maquis, the fighters for the
French federation of the FLN, who until then
had been active in the metropolis, and those,
like Ben Bella, just liberated from French jails
and thirsting for power and light. There are no women
in these ranks, which is hardly surprising given that
there were no female ministers in France either
in those days. Only men, then, men who for years had been
living for and fighting for this moment or who had
rotted in prison, brooding. Although they called each other
brother, these men had less penchant for fraternity
than most, given their ambition. Anyone who
refuses to compromise or grit their teeth and
make alliances will get nowhere; an individual
may be ever so brave and strong but still
won't stand a chance in a lion's den. Ben Bella
has many rivals and just as many enemies
in the provisional government that has yet to govern,
and so he has allied himself with the military
and its commander, Houari Boumédiène.

And so the worm is in the bud from the start, a worm
that could be compared to a boa constrictor. If your
support is the army and you're not in the military,
your perch is neither secure nor comfortable. Are there
any revolutions, foundings of states, new beginnings
without a worm? Not likely. The FLN, once a movement
in support of a free and sovereign state, becomes

a political party, in fact, the only one this new state has.
Ben Bella's plans appeal to Annette, particularly
the socialism, the nationalization of property and
the means of production, and self-government.
A third way for a developing world, as they see it. The hope
is so vast and the worm so small that it is hardly visible
to the naked eye, like a fruit fly in red wine.

On 1 July 1962, what everyone, including
de Gaulle and the French in Algeria,
has long since known or supposed is made public,
namely, the reason the referendum has been delayed
as long as possible: the vast majority
of the Algerian population – 99.72%
to be precise – no longer want to be a colony or
a part of France. Could they not have been asked
before? It took eight years of war and roughly
five hundred thousand dead, most of whom,
around four hundred and fifty thousand, were
Algerians (we will never know the exact number),
before anyone got around to asking those concerned
if, by chance, they might not prefer self-government.
It's the first time in 130 years
that they've been asked anything at all. Here in Algeria,
France is still what it was when only the clergy and
the nobility had the right to vote. Now, in 1962,
the rest are asked and the response is unanimous:
they want their own state. They probably imagine that

from now on their opinion will be sought
now and again. If so, they are mistaken.
The next time they're consulted is in 1991,
and even then their opinion is ignored.

Poor Algeria! Poor Annette. Neither knows
what they've got coming. Both are filled with hope
and great expectations for this new land,
where everything seems possible, where nothing
will stay in the same old rut. All will be new and good.
On the day before the referendum is to be held,
the three As – Annette, Amara and their friend
Abdelhamid – get in Annette's Fiat, its hot metal roof
loaded up with as many of her possessions
as it can hold, including their only frying pan,
and take the road to Algeria. Annette is running a risk
as long as Algeria is still officially a part of France,
because of her outstanding prison sentence. She is advised
not to go, but she has set her mind on returning and besides,
she must prepare for 'her' patients, who will be repatriated
before the rest of the population in exile. There are many
homeward-bound people massed along the border.
For the numerous controls, Annette has false papers
under the name Djamila Moktefi. With assumed modesty,
she lowers her head, her nose hidden behind
a very unfamiliar scarf. They cross the Morice Line
and a no man's land of barbed wire and buried mines
still redolent of death. They had set out full of joy

but now are speechless. They drive cautiously,
but they drive. The first town they reach is now
called El Aouinet but at the time still bore the name
Clairfontaine. They're welcomed with a celebration,
like the front runners of the liberating heroes, the first,
in any case, to pass since the Algerians were able
to vote for independence and for liberty. They're cheered,
embraced and kissed without restraint, Annette included,
in an atmosphere of joy and revelry.

They drive westward, on and on, until late one night
in the distance they hear a joyous sound, like the music
of euphoria. They are nearing the provincial capital
Constantine, which was founded more than a thousand years
before it was conquered by the Arabs and two thousand
years before it was captured by the French. The vibrating air
has turned the entire town into a giant soundbox
that echoes with the residents' joyful cries, sending
their cheers up to the heavens and down into the deep
ravines around the city, and to the distant outskirts,
through which Annette's Fiat slowly approaches.

Two days after the referendum, de Gaulle
has finally recognized Algeria's independence
and jubilant crowds fill the streets and alleys,
dancing to the Arabic-Andalusian music *malouf*
and to hits by Johnny Hallyday or to the twist.
Women ululate with joy the way they do

at weddings. These public celebrations
are called *liesses populaires*; the word *liesse*
comes from the Latin *laetitia*, or happiness,
but it means more, including exuberance and
contagious high spirits. Among the thousands
of people laughing and singing in celebration,
and of the countless hands waving in the air,
one suddenly grabs Annette's hand and
squeezes it. This hand belongs to Mohamed Daksi,
whom she has not seen since the trial. Before he
disappeared into prison for five years, he'd bowed
to her who had sacrificed so many years of her life
to a subjugated land, his own. Now they fall
into each other's arms, just as everyone around them
is falling into everyone else's arms, whether woman,
child or man, and regardless of religion's rules.
For these few days, joy reigns supreme.

At least, it reigns in Constantine on this particular day
that lasts roughly three days and nights, whereas
elsewhere at this time hatred and murder hold sway.
In Oran, in western Algeria, many Europeans
are massacred; the FLN and the new, provisional
police root them out of their homes, break down doors,
shoot at drivers in cars or at a woman who stepped out
onto her balcony. Many disappear, and their bodies
are never found. Next to the Rex cinema, a corpse hangs
on a meathook for a time. Elsewhere, things

are not quite as awful, but still more than bad enough.
Barely created, the country is already bathed in blood,
and not just French blood, but mostly in their own.
Algerians are murdered by Algerians because they,
like the Harkis, willingly or not, fought for the French
or simply made the mistake of getting too close
to them or just because they belonged to a rival faction.
Why does Annette take no notice of these conflicts?
In those early days in Algeria, she never feels in danger,
nor does she later; in such cases, it can be enough
to not be in those places where the violence breaks out,
to miss it all, just as in 2005, how when the *banlieues* erupted
it was easy to live in France and not see a single
car on fire when nearby, in the space of several weeks,
almost ten thousand cars were torched. You have to be
where the events are taking place and you have to want
to know about them. Does Annette want to know?

Of the million French who lived in Algeria, only
a fifth will remain. The others flee. When Annette
crosses the border in the summer of '62, most
have already left, with or without luggage,
on overcrowded boats for a country that is foreign
to them, a country called France. They *should* have
stayed, Annette thinks, they *could* have stayed.
And perhaps she thinks this because these fugitives
look like her, to the extent that Europeans
look alike and because aside from the day when

her Fiat was overturned – and that was still in Tunis –
she was never in a dangerous situation.
She finds the French Algerians' fears completely
overblown. Are they? Of course, there are those
who will stay, but they are few. It's not just that
they fear for life and limb and goods; it's simply
that their presence is unwelcome in this land where they
and sometimes their ancestors were born. Those who have
possessions will lose them all. In 2017, people are still
suing the French government for reparations.
(There is no point in trying to get anything
from Algeria – nor, it turns out, from France either.)

Perhaps one reason Annette has so little concern
about this new Algeria is that she is often
accompanied by Amara. Although not legally his wife,
she is as good as, and his presence alone protects her.
They drive from Constantine to Blida, a city
to the south of Algiers, to drop off Abdelhamid at his
home there (the same city where Frantz Fanon
had worked as head physician in a psychiatric
clinic), then they continue further south to
Berrouaghia, where Amara was born. Anyone
interested in the history of Algeria soon learns
that French Algeria was a highly stratified society
of which the highest caste, of course, were the French.
There were ties and contacts between the groups, but
they did not mix. And now that the country is finally

no longer French and the French have been sent packing,
Amara is bringing home to his parents in Berrouaghia
a woman who is not only utterly French but a good
twelve years older than he (hardly a minor detail),
and if that were not enough, she's married and has
three children (a detail we've already mentioned but which
Amara, at this point, probably has not). His elderly father
would have to welcome a foreign, adulterous Christian
as his daughter-in-law, even worse, a French, atheist
infidel. Is that not too much to ask of a devout
believer who strictly observes Islam's precepts
and laws? Annette is rather anxious as they near Amara's
parents' house in her Fiat. His oldest brother has
prepared their father somewhat, but that's small comfort.
How can she be sure of a warm welcome
when so much counts against her?

Amara's father is a wise man. His views are not as
narrow as those of many others, be they Muslim,
Christian or Jewish. His name is Mohand. His father
still fought lions, so he wasn't surprised to learn
that his sons had chased away some colonizers.
Legends slumber in his great beard and his heart
contains a large family, in the periphery of which
Annette will soon belong. She is clever and
vivacious, with eyes that are at times sky blue,
at times sea green, all characteristics bound to please
Mohand. Most important is a fact that more than

compensates for any of her faults: she has the nimbus
of a heroine from helping the FLN and got ten years
as a result. She risked – and lost – her own freedom for
Algeria's independence. That is enough to win over
not just the father but the rest of the family as well,
the entire town, in fact. After all, the brothers
had to explain the sudden appearance of a French
de facto sister-in-law somehow.

In the house, built around a large inner courtyard,
with the women living together on one side
and the men on the other, Annette gets,
for the very first time, a faint (but still very colourful)
impression of Arab family life, of the place
each member holds and the limits within which each
can move. She has entered a foreign world and
does not presume to judge. But perhaps she does?
Not judge exactly, no, she wouldn't put it that way.
Still, she can't help but react on seeing, for example,
the lovely, childless Aïcha's sad face when her husband
brings a young rival into the family.
Because of her medical degree and her support
of the FLN, Annette plays a kind of hybrid role
between man and woman for the weeks of her visit.
In the women's eyes, she's a peculiar kind of woman,
and the men see her as a peculiar kind of man.
She's the only woman allowed to eat with the men
if she'd like; she's also the only woman allowed to sit

with Mohand when he rests in the shade of the fig tree
with an eye on the sheep grazing nearby. Is Annette
thinking of the future? As we have said, the worm
is in the bud of the new, independent Algerian state,
but it's also in the bud of her new love: Amara
is becoming someone else in this new, free land,
and besides, passion denotes great suffering
as well as overpowering desire. Berrouaghia!
Maybe things will work out after all.

After the joy of being reunited, the lovers leave
for Algiers. Their mission now is to make of Algeria
a beautiful country. Annette is no tourist this time.
What is she then? She must live and work here. Here?
It's so terribly foreign to her. Everything she did,
which earned her a sentence of ten years, she did for this
    country
and for people whose qualities and characteristics
she barely knows. In other words: she acted on principle,
not for the sake of this particular country's culture,
customs, languages, religions and regions.
She considers Camus a good writer and a truly good man,
but unlike him she places principle over individual
cases, all the more so since she knows almost no
individuals here. She has only just arrived.

While the two lovers are in Blida and Berrouaghia,
the struggle for power is quickly decided

high above their heads: the provisional government,
which had previously led all negotiations with the French,
ended up being far more provisional than it had hoped.
Others have captured the crown, namely the military
arm of the FLN stationed at the borders, which,
unlike the decimated partisans in the Maquis,
emerged stronger from the war under the command
of Colonel Boumédiène. The colonel knows
that in this time of transition he cannot lead alone
and therefore needs someone he can manipulate.
He chooses the socialist Ben Bella, whom Annette knows
from Tunisia. Of course, the story can be told from another
angle in which Ben Bella leans on the colonel to govern.
But one thing is certain from the very first day:
the army and Ben Bella are in the same boat,
even if the rudder is not initially in their hands.

Annette sits in that boat as well, but as a passenger
not fully aware of the destination. Now nearing forty,
she has long dreamed of a country in which socialism
does not connote Soviet gulag rule but genuine fraternity,
a country in which citizens share their wealth and govern
together. In France, that ideal no longer has a hope, but
why not here, in this newborn land with few industries
and no lobbies? Aren't all possibilities still imaginable
and open here? One possibility that is realized
is a position in the administration for Annette,
in the Ministry of Health to be precise, and there

she interacts with people she would not have greeted
a short time ago. Looking back from the distant future,
which is the present for her and for us, she sees herself
with some astonishment and some shame, but at the time
she saw only the country's great potential and its
enormous needs due to a woeful lack of doctors
(even fewer than under French rule) and its panoply
of diseases: tuberculosis, typhus, cholera,
not to mention famine. Saving lives and alleviating
suffering, not just in individual cases
as every doctor does, but through general
measures, like countrywide vaccines, training
doctors and nurses – is there any negative side
to such efforts? Are these political acts
or acts of kindness? Is she driven by ambition
or devotion? The answer isn't clear – and besides,
what difference does it make? Aren't the outcomes
most important?

From this point on, nights are few and far between,
if night is defined by rest, recovery or sleep.
There are so many things to set right, so terribly much
to accomplish, that forty-eight-hour days wouldn't
be enough, not even months or years would suffice.
Like Sisyphus, Annette is prepared to roll her rock
uphill, but her mountain is so enormous, she cannot see
the peak: where to start? First, new doctors must be found;
almost all the old ones left for France. Many of the archives and

hospitals have been destroyed by those who left, a gesture
　　that,
in the language of the fanatics among the *Pieds-Noirs*,
willing up to the very end to use murderous means
to hold on to their colony, signified: We're leaving,
fine, that's what you wanted. But first, we'll tear
everything down and you all can go to hell.

In the new ministry, Annette is put in charge of
education and research. 'Her' minister is a man,
Nekkache, whom she knows from Tunisia,
where he oversaw care of the wounded and ill
in the border troops of the Algerian army.
As earlier with Ben Bella, Annette's sense
of Nekkache – a doctor who, rumour has it, treats
indigent patients free of charge – is that he is not
a bad man. Indeed, she sees that he spares no effort
to improve all lives. He doesn't seem to be after
honours or money but is striving instead for
a better world, and for him 'better' means a world
in which fewer children die. Such is Annette's
impression of the man and she most likely doesn't know,
no, she could not be aware, that during the Second
World War Nekkache was recruited by the Abwehr,
Germany's military intelligence service, and he remained
in contact until the 1950s with Richard Christmann,
an Abwehr agent in France under the Nazis and
after the war an agent with the BND, West Germany's

foreign intelligence service. To all appearances,
during the years of proclaimed Franco-German friendship,
Adenauer's Germany covertly supported the FLN,
in other words, a group France had declared
a terrorist organization.

This is what you can see if you look closely,
which is, paradoxically, easier to do
from a distance or, at least, if you're not buried,
like Annette, in the sands of the present. What we see
is that in these times almost everyone has something
to hide, at least among those who are in or want power,
even if the ends they want to serve are good:
education and equal rights for all, work and
decent healthcare. This is true of Nekkache, a rather
unimposing man, and it is no doubt also true
of the charming Ben Bella, who has his enemies
and rivals put in prison – as others in his shoes
surely would have – and who manages very quickly
to become not only president but also head of the sole
political party and then, to cement his complete control,
names himself Minister of the Interior.
This is true and does not escape Annette, but she
wants so ardently for this new beginning,
this social restructuring, to succeed. She also sees
the feuds between the power-hungry men and
the different factions – frankly, who could contain these
ambitions and rivalries but a benevolent dictator

who would later cede his place to more or less
democratic structures once they are established
enough to endure? Because, compared to those
who could be in his place, BB seems to Annette
relatively honest and benign, and what he wants
to achieve (and has already made some progress towards)
is a socialism of the Yugoslavian variety, not the Soviet,
the kind of socialism, that is, of which Annette
has long dreamed and which ultimately is probably
more suited to dreams than to reality.

Democracy? Could someone please explain how
that is supposed to work from one day to the next
in a country in which the vast majority is illiterate
because for the past 130 years the State didn't consider
literacy necessary? Where can one form a free opinion
in casting one's vote if not from printed material?
Of course, the Algerians understood the question
of whether or not they wanted independence very well
without being able to read or write. But voters are rarely
presented with such clear alternatives. Auguste Blanqui,
the socialist and patron saint of today's ultra-left,
whose motto *No gods, no masters* Annette adopted
as her own, believed eight decades earlier that revolution
should be followed by a dictatorship for one or ten years
because those subjugated to centuries of tyranny
must first learn how to think and learn how to be free.
What Blanqui did not explain was how to get rid of

the dictators again after a year or a decade of their rule.
Lord Macaulay – before Blanqui – had a different view.
His belief that a people should be given liberty only once
they have learned how to use it recalls the fable
of the fool who refused to get in the water until
he had learned how to swim.

A single-party state? All the decision-making
power clenched in one hand? Annette is sometimes
uneasy when she considers this, but she has
more immediate concerns than these power struggles.
There is a population of nearly eleven million
men, women and children, many of whom are
sick and starving, and here are a hundred doctors,
three hundred at the very most. What difference
does it make if someone in the government has got
his claws into three ministries? Annette works.
For three years, she does nothing else.

Isn't this as if one of us Europeans, a German or
an Italian, suddenly decided to develop and manage
the education or healthcare system of, say,
Bolivia? Isn't she lost in a country she barely knows,
a land three quarters desert and four times the size
of her own, where nearly all those in need of medical
care speak a mysterious language with sounds
formed for the most part deep in the throat?

Yes and no. On the one hand, many of the government
and cabinet officials feel just as lost as Annette,
since they were soldiers, prisoners or students
in France (actual France, not one of its colonies)
and therefore don't know large parts of their own
vast country any better than she. Who among them
showed any interest in the region of Kabylia
or in nomadic life in the Sahara? More than a few
speak much better French than Arabic. Still,
there's something else. They strike Annette as
irreligious, secular French, and above all socialist,
yet they've absorbed something that makes this land
and its inhabitants more familiar to them than to her,
and these are customs, traditions and religion.
It must be noted that Annette will not see or try to
understand the importance that religion will have and
to some extent already does (that is, the kind
of religion that doesn't distinguish between
mysticism and politics and is widely promoted
for the sense of unity it fosters) because she
doesn't want to see it. It wouldn't be the first time
someone closed their eyes to what doesn't fit
the picture they want to see. We've all done this.

She is and remains a foreigner and doesn't always
have the skills she needs, but after eight years of war,
destruction and the loss of countless doctors,
teachers, journalists and so on, everyone is needed.

Even under the French, the educated were few and
far between, and since they disproportionately joined
the underground or the Maquis, many were
eliminated – not by the French, at least not directly,
to the extent that the French secret service skilfully
made certain Algerians look suspicious to the FLN.
And the latter were stupid or gullible enough to
dispatch them (to France's delight) in paranoid purges
of their own ranks. As a result, in 1962 they need
absolutely anyone with any education and goodwill,
from home or abroad.

Hang on: wasn't independence the idea?
Weren't the Algerians finally to govern themselves?
Yes, indeed. But in these early days of independence,
someone who served the FLN and was imprisoned
for it is more Algerian than, say, someone from
Sidi bel Abbès who did nothing or, worse, worked
for the French. As proof of this and to her great surprise,
Annette is offered Algerian citizenship
in November '62 by the new president himself,
Ben Bella. What to do? For Annette,
one nationality is more than enough.
She's dedicated instead to socialism and
internationalism. On top of that,
she doesn't feel Algerian in the least, much less
Muslim. Still, it's a gift and she can hardly refuse
to accept it with her thanks. She is naturalized

on 1 November, on All Saints' Day and Algeria's first
national holiday, their Bastille Day, so to speak,
because on this day in '54 everything began.
Insurrection. Revolution. Algeria's independence.

A brief digression: the Bastille, a dark dungeon,
as everyone knows, held mostly aristocrats,
often at the request of their own families, who,
for various reasons, wanted them out of the way.
In 1789, the Bastille held only seven prisoners.
In 1954, during the 1 November attacks, four French
civilians were killed – a forester, two young teachers
and a taxi driver – along with three soldiers, an officer
and two Algerians. And this is the day they choose
to celebrate? It's clear that national holidays do not
commemorate what happened on a given date
but what is associated with that day, a symbol
of liberation or rebirth that may have nothing or
as good as nothing to do with historical events,
regardless of who or how many died or were freed.

While Annette and many others recently come
from around the world, especially the so-called
developing world, spare no work or effort, clouds gather
overhead. In their shapes, from our vantage today
we can distinguish faces and, behind these faces,
the army, specifically the border army of the FLN.
At the time, no one realizes exactly what this arm

of the military is and will remain: the only victor.
On the one hand there is the face, as long and sharp
as a blade, of the future traitor Boumédiène, who
commanded these soldiers and consequently is now
Ben Bella's defence minister and vice president.
On the other hand there is the face, as wide
as it is high, of a short man of twenty-five, who
will be ruling his country fifty years later
from his wheelchair and from sickbeds in
French and Swiss hospitals. He, too, was in
the border army, and his start as Minister for Youth
and Sport and for Tourism seems oddly harmless,
as a dictator can when still in his chrysalis.
His tourism portfolio, in any case, will hardly
keep him chained to his desk. Who on earth
would want to holiday in Algeria at this time?

The war is over; the war continues. Many
are murdered. Still, there are those who brave
the dangers, sympathizers, supporters and…
Annette's mother, Petite Marthe, now
in her sixties. Her only daughter left Le Guildo,
the backwater town on the Arguenon estuary,
to protect the world from all evils and to heal it.
She is now a part of a government on the other side
of the Mediterranean and Petite Marthe wants to know
how things are there and if her daughter is getting

  enough

food and sleep. So Petite Marthe packs her bag
and sets out for Algeria. While hundreds of thousands
of Europeans are fleeing, she fearlessly swims against
the tide. Annette is very busy and sometimes brings
her mother along so she can see some of
this foreign land. One day they're driving along,
the chauffeur napping in the back seat while,
as so often, Annette sits at the wheel and chats
with Petite Marthe, when a car roars past, horn blaring,
then cuts them off so abruptly that Annette has to stop.
She gives her fury full vent until she recognizes
the man getting out of the insolent car as Ben Bella.
Hearty greetings and introductions all around.
Petite Marthe meets the president.

Where they've stopped, there's a café on one side
of the street and French army barracks on the other,
since the Évian Accords provide only for the staged
withdrawal of French forces over the next two years.
Everyone gets out of the cars for a drink in the café,
which is full of French soldiers. Look! The president!
They crowd around Ben Bella and shake his hand.
They're honoured, having apparently forgotten
that not so long ago this man was serving time
in a French prison as a terrorist and a danger
to the State. In no time at all, with a title
and an office, a convict can be president.

It's all very simple, and terribly complicated.
Simple because there are no regulations
guiding administrative and government
procedures. Each person deals with whatever
is most urgent whenever and wherever they can,
at the home of a minister or the president,
night or day. What gives Annette the feeling that she's
in the right place with the right kind of people are
circumstances that others might consider secondary:
the friendly, informal relations among government
officials, their simple lifestyle and lack of
self-importance. Minister of Health Nekkache,
for example, lives in a three-room apartment.

It may be an advantage or a weakness, but
Annette is very susceptible to… how to put it?
Perhaps it's captured best by a person's character,
their nature, the impression they have on her. Are they
sincere? Are they what they seem? Nationalization
of large properties, self-determination,
socialism – she approves and believes they are
the best solutions. But if it weren't for Ben Bella,
Nekkache and a few others she trusts, she would never
have been part of this government. Is she deluding
    herself?
Or rather, are there many things she didn't notice or
only noticed later and much too late?

She has an uncomfortable sense of déjà vu,
and to escape it she throws herself into her work.
What was the Resistance if not a struggle for liberation
from an occupying force? And what are occupiers
if not colonizers? In her mind, the two are the same
kind of resistance, only this time her country
is the occupying force. The second parallel
is that she sees the struggle for liberation
as synonymous with upheaval. The occupiers
are forced out and a new society is established.
Why had they fought if the exploiters are simply
to be replaced with others? In 1945, victory was stolen
from the communists, in Annette's view, because
the country that materialized after the war was not
the one for which they'd risked their lives. And now?
Around her, she sees a new bourgeoisie, Algerian
this time, and the old clans grabbing all the privileges.
Nekkache and Ben Bella are different. She clings
to this conviction and anxiously overlooks the rest.

Annette has her work and she has love. Not bad at all!
A great many don't have either. But does she have love
or does love have her? A change is gradually taking over
Amara. He looks at her differently, his gaze more distant,
when he sees her at all, since she is often on the road,
assessing the level of health around the country. Her trips
take her to remote corners, to oases where hardly anyone
speaks French, so she always brings an interpreter.

She learns the gestures of the desert people. She tries to learn
Arabic, too, but gives up after a great effort – she has far less
talent for languages than for revolution. Amara is also
often on the move. With his friends. His work
in a ministry lasted only as long as it was based
abroad, in Tunisia, and the nation not yet established.
Now there is an official state, Amara doesn't want to serve,
doesn't want a position and especially doesn't want a boss
that he dislikes but has to tolerate. The ministry
in the provisional government where he had worked
was that of 'general liaison', espionage
in other words. After independence, Boussouf was replaced
as head by Boumédiène. The Boussouf Boys, who are
not as harmless as the name makes them seem,
are not welcome in the new state. They're stripped
of a leader whom Ben Bella has sidelined
with the help and to the benefit of another. Some
of the boys end up shifting to the secret police
and Boumédiène's service. Not Amara.
He doesn't trust the new head. Maybe he had hoped
for too much from independence, expecting solutions
to many, even all, difficult problems, and after
the first transports of joy, the raptures that follow victory,
Amara was filled with disappointment.
In addition to this, as so often happens, after the first
phase of a relationship when love, love, love
rules the day, one person who is a certain way
emerges from the mist as someone completely

different. An easy explanation for this is 'cultural
background', even though what is being evoked
doesn't hover in the background but lies deep within
each person. Moreover, Annette has a high position
and he has none. To be sure, he doesn't want one,
but the imbalance is not ideal for his ego. And finally
there are her two marriages and probably more than
two lovers as well. Until now, Annette has lived
as women a generation or two younger will. Amara
is filled with jealousy and makes terrible scenes.
He smashes things to bits (but does not hurt her).
And then one day it's over. Without warning,
Amara leaves Annette.

She feels as if she has fallen into a deep crater – there was
something about this man that, fifty years later, she still
cannot forget, a mystery that is sparked between skin and
    skin
and between two pairs of eyes but rarely has a future.
It flares up and leaves embers that, in severe cases
like this one, will smoulder for an entire life.

She had her work and she had love. The work she still has,
and she has more and more of it, the less love she has.
With her colleagues, Annette is battling the spread of
trachoma, a bacterial infection that can lead to blindness,
and the other diseases running rampant in this country,
while she herself is suffering another kind of blindness,

against which there is no other treatment than
a bucket of cold water, which she receives full face
the morning of 19 June 1965.

Someone telephones her at five in the morning and
hangs up without saying hello. A wrong number?
Or did someone want to know if she's at home?
Annette doesn't have time to fall back asleep before
the telephone rings again. This time it's a good friend
who not only does say hello but also something about
tanks in the streets. For several days they've been filming
in the centre of Algiers, the movie mentioned earlier
that reconstitutes the Battle of Algiers to the music
of Ennio Morricone and Bach. For the shoot, multiple tanks
drive through the streets, and the army used the opportunity
to advance discreetly to the edge of the medina
in real tanks. The friend on the other end of the line
finds the movements of the troops highly suspicious.
Annette agrees with him completely because the penny
has suddenly dropped (or a heavy curtain has lifted), and
she perceives what she chose not to see in recent months:
Colonel's Boumédiène's knife-like profile and Minister
Abdelaziz Bouteflika's squint. They're part
of the Oujda clan, who were pushed out of power
by Ben Bella and have no intention of ceding
authority they consider rightly theirs, especially
since they have tanks and, consequently, greater strength.

Annette throws on a skirt and is out of her house
by ten past five. Where should she go? She hears
that Ben Bella and Nekkache have been arrested.
She herself is in no little danger of the same. She
goes through all the friends she has. Her admirers, too.
One of them drops her off in front of the magnificent
home of a parasitologist, but she changes her mind
and decides instead to go to the Ds', whose garden
offers access to the grounds of the British embassy
through an underground chapel, just in case.
Conveniently, the Ds will be leaving on holiday
in two days. It seems odd to go away
during a military coup, but that is their plan.
Annette has the apartment to herself and nothing
to do but wait and brood. All that she has done
or failed to do over the past six years
runs continuously through her mind and
weighs on her chest like a heavy stone.

For five weeks, Annette is alone. During the day,
she stays in the two rooms that are not visible
from outside. She spends the nights on the walled-in
terrace with a narrow view of the star-filled sky
that gives answers only to those who know how
to read the constellations. Food and newspapers
are brought by a few friends privy to her secret, and
she is kept aware of who has been arrested and who
is still free – for now. She also has a radio to which she can

listen in the windowless bathroom. Long stretches
of military music are interrupted now and again
with the latest news: Algeria has been freed
from the dangerous tyrant and his Trotskyite advisers,
most of whom were foreigners. Well then. True,
Ben Bella had amassed too much power, but
it's still remarkable to hear the charge coming from
the head of the army, who has just overthrown
the president and has no intention of returning power
to the people. This self-proclaimed leader was poised
to remain at the helm for all eternity, until Death,
the only one more powerful in the land, dethroned him
fourteen years later in the guise of Waldenström's
disease (yet one more treacherous foreigner;
you see, you can never be too wary.)

Annette does not plan on staying that long. After
several weeks of self-imposed solitary confinement,
she has had enough of herself and the country,
and more than enough of the stars and illusions.
What on earth has she done? And for what?
Independence? Liberty? For tanks to be stationed
on every corner? For everyone to be too intimidated
to open their mouths? Did she lose her three children,
Myriam, newly hatched, and Gilles and Jean-Henri,
so that a military regime could subject Algeria
to a reign of terror? Can that be?

It cannot be, because it must not be. Surely Annette
now recognizes that something was wrong from the start,
from the birth of this long-awaited nation; the political
orientation, the ideological bent seemed to play less of a role
than the clans and certain people. Her president, the one
she gave all her support, knew how to steer his boat, but
could not maintain the course alone, not without making a
    deal
with the Devil. He was certainly no angel. And yet
at one point there was a provisional government,
an opposition with Ferhat Abbas, Krim Belkacem,
Boudiaf... What has become of them?
Condemned to death, imprisoned, forced into exile.

She told herself that it couldn't have been otherwise
after so much oppression for such a long time;
technically they were in France, but democracy
is something else and now they're supposed to master
a system of just representation from one day to the next?
Those who look for excuses will always find them,
and when one is oneself on the oppressors' side – not
Annette personally, of course, but her country – there is
a tendency to justify the vices and mistakes
of the formerly oppressed.

In her hiding place, Annette's only tendency
is to see the truth to which she had been blind and now
must face for the first time in ages. That truth

is unbearable: she has forfeited her three children
for the sake of a sovereign state that, in a very short time,
in just three years, has turned into a military dictatorship,
which it will remain for decades, although
she fortunately cannot know this yet.

It is late. Too late, of course. Many made mistakes,
but the consequences of these errors were not the same
for everyone. Some did not survive. Others managed
to turn their mistake, bit by bit, to good, becoming wiser.
Not Annette. Her mistake becomes a painful burden
she rolls up the hill that is her life, a hill that grows
into a mountain, and each time she thinks she has reached
the peak, she finds hidden behind it a still higher ridge
that she must scale with her burden. This anguish
will last the better part of a century in all.

Thanks to a stylish new dress given to her
by the embassy attaché from Ghana and thanks
to the protection of a few loyal friends and lawyer,
Georges Kiejman, who arrived to free her from this trap,
and thanks especially to her good fortune, at the end
of a long summer Annette is able to disappear from
the country for which she had set out to fight and found
and for the sake of which she had to bear imprisonment
and exile. Now it's all over. Farewell Algeria!
Farewell hope, self-determination and communal sharing!

Those who wanted progress are now brought to heel. This
reining in began under Ben Bella, Algeria's first president, who
will spend more years in house arrest in his independent
    country
than he had under the hated colonizers. Almost his entire
cabinet changes sides to the new strongman,
which not only reveals the level of their loyalty but also
shows that this coup d'état was not about
establishing a new political structure, it was just
a changing of the guard. Grabbing power, privileges.
The Benbellists are caught, true, but it turns out
that they are surprisingly few,
far fewer, at least, than before.

Where now for Annette? Her parents' country
will be closed to her for years until an amnesty
puts an end to her exile, and her second nationality,
recently imposed on her, is also of no use.
Why not Rome? She passed through it on her way here
and will pass through it again on her way to Vienna
(where she'll attend a neurological conference on the way),
then Switzerland. Geneva was the first step of her escape
and perhaps her last, as she will stay here despite
receiving several offers. She turns down an invitation
from Cuba, for example, because she wants,
in her words, 'to preserve one small nook of illusion',
and she is offered an interesting position at the hospital.
In the Swiss Confederation there is little risk

of a military coup for the foreseeable future,
but that factor does not weigh heavily in her decision.

Of all the places she is allowed to reside outside of
France, where she is still on the wanted list, Geneva
is the closest to Marseille and, therefore, to her children,
aside from Turin, perhaps, and San Remo, but
she has no job offers there. Geneva it is then.
The university medical centre. Peace and quiet
at last. But no! Not even! There will be new attempts
to improve the world, less spectacular, to be sure,
but still much more than what the rest of us do
in a lifetime. Here we'll leap forward forty, fifty years,
as is only possible in the mind or on paper,
leaving behind us decades of real life
that shrink in memory. But before jumping ahead
to the next century, the next millennium even,
a brief remark about the children: although
a long prison sentence awaits her if she's caught,
Annette often travels to France from Geneva
using false papers so that she can hug her children
here and there, in the homes of friends, their substitute
parents or at boarding schools. Each time, she is torn
by the same indescribable pain that comes from the sense
that she has become a stranger to her children.

The children will grow up. Far from their mother,
they will live their lives and two will die before her.

The rock Annette must roll uphill grows heavier
and the crest higher. Under the burden, her back
begins to curve. Her hair is white and her eyes
now alternate between light green and the blue
of winter sky. Her medical practice and her research
come to an end and, finally pardoned, she returns
to France. For the past three decades, she has lived
in a narrow house in Dieulefit, in the Drôme
in south-eastern France. It's not far from Vercors, where
many from the Resistance hid during the Occupation,
which was mostly under Italian forces and therefore
less severe. Of the many who found refuge in Dieulefit,
not one was denounced. Annette chose
to settle here because she passed through
on her bicycle one day in 1944 and took a shine
to it. Her choice had nothing to do with
what happened here or didn't – the lack
of denunciations – but it was probably not
a coincidence either.

Whether 'God-made-it' or it was made by someone else,
this village is where she now lives, short, bent and alone.
Only slightly bent and only externally;
internally, she is as upright as ever, as upright
as anyone can be in this world. In her small car,
she is still criss-crossing all of France, driving
thousands of kilometres to Brittany to visit friends
in Saint-Cast and often to schools to teach children

when and how to disobey. Soon she will be
one hundred years old.

One November afternoon, she goes to a film preview
in Dieulefit to see a German documentary by Malte Ludin
called *Two or Three Things I Know About Him*, with
subtitles. It is followed by a panel discussion, the kind
where people discuss things they know nothing about.
When the panel is done opining, the floor is opened
to the audience. Annette rises to speak and her words
fill the hall and captivate the room. Among
those captivated is a tall, serious German woman
on the podium with the expression of someone
who has suddenly realized that it's time to listen,
not talk. That evening there is a dinner for those
who have lasted until the end. The restaurant
is full and loud. It's a weekend night. Annette
is enjoying the duck breast. Without any ulterior
motive, the tall German sitting next to her
savours a dish of spaghetti in squid ink sauce.

She listens to Annette's story – an abbreviated
version – without the slightest intention
of writing it down someday. She has nothing
in mind, or very little, because she must concentrate
so hard to hear what Annette is saying over
the clinking glasses, clattering cutlery and roar
of voices. She looks at Annette intently and can hardly

believe her eyes: You actually exist? You're real?
The German woman *sees* Annette speak almost
as much as she hears her, so lively and friendly
to the stranger at her table. But what
does 'stranger' mean – that's exactly the point.
No human is a stranger to another, but very few
behave accordingly. What strikes the woman
listening so intently is Annette's way of speaking,
rapidly, half-swallowing some syllables, with a bit
of argot and idiomatic expressions all her own,
all in all very differently than doctors usually
speak. One turn of phrase, for example, pops up
again and again. Where others would say
si tu veux (if you'd like) or *si tu préfères*
(if you'd prefer), Annette has a penchant for
using a personal idiom: if you'd like to go there,
si tu veux aller par là.

The woman with the dish of squid in ink
experiences that evening what in other circumstances
might be called a *coup de foudre*, a flash
of love at first sight. Soon after she gets home,
she returns to Dieulefit to visit Annette,
who offers her a bed and meals, as she has
to so many. And Annette talks to her.

After a while and according to its nature,
the squid begins to secrete its black ink,

filling the place it had just been. What remains
is a black cloud, and in this cloud's fine, black
lines Annette comes to life, white and blue.

Camus was a pacifist; Annette was not.
And yet her existence illuminates something
he wrote. All we need to do is substitute her name
for Sisyphus in the following passage:
'In that subtle moment when a man looks back
over his life, Sisyphus, returning to his rock,
contemplates the succession of unrelated actions
that becomes his fate, created by him,
united in his memory's gaze and sealed by his death.
The struggle itself towards the summit is enough
to fill a man's heart. We must imagine Sisyphus happy.'

This book is based on Anne Beaumanoir's oral accounts of her life and on her memoir, *Le Feu de la mémoire* (The Fire of Memory), published in 2000 by Éditions Bouchène.

The Rhythm of a Life

When considering how best to convey Annette Beaumanoir's remarkable life, Anne Weber realized that the ancient, disused form of the heroic epic would allow her to find a fruitful distance from her subject's real life. Telling Annette's story in free verse let Weber exploit the tension between the sweeping historical panorama of the epic and the unusual heroism in the ordinary, individual life of a woman from a humble background. There are, in this narrative poem, a variety of linguistic registers and tones: at times the diction is elevated, as befits an epos, at times it is colloquial, particularly when Annette's words are quoted, and occasionally it is wry, even sardonic, especially when the narrative voice intrudes on the tale.

Capturing these shifts in tone, the rhythmic flow of the language and the emphases and dramatic pauses of the line breaks was challenging enough, but my task as a translator was further complicated (yet also enriched) by the fact that I was working from two versions of the work. Weber wrote the first version of *Annette* in German and, rather than translate it into French, she wrote a new version in her second language. There are some discrepancies, a few extra lines here, a few lines omitted there, cultural markers or historical events with which German readers are familiar are given an explanation or additional context for French readers and vice versa. In triangulating between the German, French and English versions, my first priority was rhythmic consistency. Each language has its particular rhythm and its rules governing word order, and my aim was always to maintain a rhythmic and syntactical flow in English that reads as naturally as both the French and the German versions do. In more than one passage, I took elements from each version and fused them into the English lines.

The quote from Petr Alekseevich Kropotkin's *Memoirs of a Revolutionist* is taken from the 1899 Houghton Mifflin, which does not name the translator.

I would like to thank Anne Weber for her generosity and patience in answering my questions. I would also like to express my gratitude to the Europäisches Übersetzer-Kolloquium in Straelen for convening an online conference with Anne and eight of her translators for three days of insightful and meticulous exchanges on the challenges and joys of translating *Epic Annette*.

—TESS LEWIS

The author would like to thank everyone
who helped to publish *Epic Annette*.

THE INDIGO PRESS TEAM

Susie Nicklin
Phoebe Barker
Honor Scott

JACKET DESIGN

Luke Bird

PUBLICITY

Claire Maxwell

EDITORIAL PRODUCTION

Tetragon
Sarah Terry
Bryan Karetnyk

And especially Tess Lewis, who translated it marvellously.